Writing Tips

Volume 1

Exploring the Writer's Path

Creative Talents Unleashed

GENERAL INFORMATION

Writing Tips

By

Creative Talents Unleashed

1st Edition: 2016

This Publishing is protected under Copyright Law as a "Collection". All rights for all submissions are retained by the Individual Author and or Artist. No part of this publishing may be Reproduced, Transferred in any manner without the prior **WRITTEN CONSENT** of the "Material Owner" or it's Representative Creative Talents Unleashed.

www.ctupublishinggroup.com

Publisher Information
1st Edition: Creative Talents Unleashed
CreativeTalentsUnleashed@aol.com
www.ctupublishinggroup.com

This Collection is protected under U.S. and International Copyright laws

Copyright © 2016 Creative Talents Unleashed

ISBN-13: 978-0692640340 (Creative Talents Unleashed)
ISBN-10: 0692640347

$15.95

Credits

Cover

Donna J. Sanders

Contributors

Donna J. Sanders

Jody Austin

Laura Marie Clark

Raja Williams

Introduction

Donna J. Sanders

Photography

Donna J. Sanders

Raja Williams

Dedication

With loving hearts the writers featured in *Writing Tips Volume 1 Exploring The Writer's Path* donated their writing for this publishing to help establish a starving artist fund for writers that may not be able to financially afford the fees of becoming a published author. All proceeds from this publication are being donated to said fund. With that being said, this book is for all the aspiring writers out there. Keep your dream alive and keep working toward it daily.

For More Information Please Visit:

www.ctupublishinggroup.com/starving-artist-fund.html

Writing Tip

Creative Talents Unleashed
www.creativetalentsunleashed.info

Introduction

Do you dream of being a writer? Have you already dabbled with words, but still need some help finding your style on paper? Or are you one of those who have so much to write, but just can't find the time to get the task done? This book could be your saving grace. Put together by a group of talented writers from the Creative Talents Unleashed family, Writing Tips Vol. 1 is for any level of writer.

I believe everyone can write. If you can carry on a simple conversation, then you are capable of writing. Some just don't know where to start. You don't have to be educated or have a degree to be a good writer. Some of the greatest writers in the world didn't have that opportunity when they started writing. If you've written in a journal or a letter, you're already an author. You just have to find the passion and motivation to write. This book covers a little bit of everything a writer needs from start to finish.

If you are one of the fortunate parents with a student who loves to read and write, there are many guidelines to get a young writer started. From using online resources and social media as a tool, to focusing on the five senses; Writing Tips explores many avenues to keep a teenage mind occupied.

Juggling college and a job takes patience and determination. Both may require some writing skills that you need to hone. There are articles on forms, grammar and how to strengthen your abilities as a writer. Jody Austin breaks down several poetic forms with examples, for those aspiring poets. But you don't have to be a poet or major in English Literature to enjoy the book. The tips included can be used for everyday tasks like writing a simple letter, a grant proposal or even a class essay.

How many of us are often limited on time because of our responsibilities with our full-time jobs and raising families? There are barely enough hours in the day to take care of ourselves, much less attempt to write. Our authors share some creative ways to utilize your time to write. Whether you are waiting for hours at a doctor's appointment or suffering from a sleepless night, there are many moments that can be used productively to put some words on paper.

For those who have lived a full life, enjoying retirement, and finally escaped the chaos of a crowded city, there are quite a few writing tips for you if you have decided to journal your experiences. You now have to time to "Write a Little Every Day" as Laura Clark suggests. You have more of an opportunity to observe people and nature around you. Solitude is a most helpful writing tool, and this is your chance to use it for your benefit.

If writing is just a fun hobby or maybe just your therapy, there are many key points to aid you. For writers who just enjoy it, there are some tips for thinking outside the box, to experiment with styles never tried before. For those using it to de-stress, our authors share their methods using writing to reach out to others who may be suffering in the same way. If you are ready to share your work with others, Raja Williams delves into where to submit and offers some valuable publishing tips.

Whether you are just a lover of literature or want to take your writing to the next step, Writing Tips will be an informative and delightful read. This book will fit perfectly in a classroom, use it as a coffee table book to create a few conversations, or give it to friend who is struggling with their writing. It was written by writers who enjoy their craft, with the hope of motivating and inspiring others to enjoy the art of writing.

Donna J. Sanders

Table of Contents

Dedication	v
Introduction	vii

Get In The Writing Mindset

Get in the Writing Mindset	2
Write a Little Every Day	3
Begin With What You Know	4
Find Your Writing Space	6
Writing Tools	7
Writing Ideas	9
Creativity Comes First	10
If It Doesn't Work, Move On	11
Dare To Put Yourself Out There	12
Writing For Personal Fulfilment	13
What Should I Write About?	14
Engage With Others In Your Position	15
Staying Motivated	16

Table of Contents . . . continued

Stuck? Try Something New

Stuck? Try Something New	20
Take Advantage of Prompts	21
Music as Inspiration	22
Observing People	23
Using Words	25
Listen With Everything	27
Expand Your Vocabulary . . . But Don't Overuse Long or Obscure Words	29
There Are Great Characters Out There (In The Real World)	30
Use The Unusual Details	31
Creating Strong Emotions	33
Be A Witness	34
Leave Your Most Powerful Image For Last	35

Grammar

Colon and Semicolon	38

Table of Contents . . . continued

Too and To (and Two)	39
It's vs. Its	40
There, They're and Their	41
Adverbs	42
Watch Your Tenses	43
Metaphor and Simile	44
Alliteration	45
Assonance	46
Vary the Length of Your Sentences	47
Onomatopoeia	48

Think Small . . . Write Big

Think Small . . . Write Big	50
A Season of Delicious Thoughts	52
Different Types of Writing Can Benefit You	55
Missed Opportunities	57
Stories in the Media	58
Senses	59

Table of Contents . . . continued

Listen to Your Words	61
Set Realistic Targets	62
Pruning The Weeds	63
Obsessions Have Power	65
From Trash To Treasure	67
Revitalize The World	69
A Classic Story Finds Life Again	71
An Epic Lesson	73
Graveyard Poetry	75
A Love For Literature	77

Let Your Poetry Be Open To Interpretation

Let Your Poetry Be Open To Interpretation	82
Poetry: Know Your Purpose	83
To Rhyme Or Not To Rhyme?	84
Poetry: How Long is a Line?	85
Rhythm in Poetry	87
Playful Poetry	88

Table of Contents . . . continued

Repetition in Poetry	90
Concrete Words and Images	91
Visual Poetry	92
We All Write Bad Poems	94
8 Essential Tips for Crafting and Sharing Your Poetry	95

Poetry Forms

Form: Free Verse Poetry	98
Prose Poetry	99
Response Poems	100
Freestyle Poetry	102
Elegy	103
Ode	104
Form: Haiku	105
Form: Hay Na Ku	106
Form: Tanka	107
Form: Cinquain	108
Form: Tetractys	109

Table of Contents . . . continued

Form: Etheree	110
Form: Nonet	112
Form: 6 Word Story	114

Tips to Strengthen the Writer

Continuity	116
Use Active Voice	118
Eliminate Unnecessary Words	119
Read Your Writing Aloud	120
Editing Your Writing	121
The Importance of Background Research	122
Using Images	123
Beginning and Ending	124
Ask For Specific Feedback	125
Know Your Target Audience	126
Blog Etiquette - Poetry & Pictures	127
Raise Your Voice	130
Social Media: Personal vs. Professional Pages	132

Table of Contents . . . continued

Handling Rejection	135
Give A Book	136

After You're Published-What Happens Next?

After You're Published – What Happens Next?	140
The Obstacles We Face as Writers	142
Choosing The Right Poems For Publishing	145
Anthologies – Should I or Shouldn't I Submit My Work?	147
When is The Best Time For an Author to Release a Second or Third Book?	150
I asked a Friend to Write My Books Foreword	151
I Dedicate This Book To . . .	152
Marketing Yourself – Don't Leave Out Important Information	154
Why a Book Review is Important	158
Reasons Why You Should Join a Writing Group	160
About the Authors	164
Starving Artist Fund	168
Our Links	169

Writing Tips

Volume 1

Exploring the Writer's Path

Creative Talents Unleashed

Get In The Writing Mindset

Get in the Writing Mindset

Sometimes, you are not in the right mindset to write anything productive. It does not matter whether you want to write a haiku or a full length novel: you are not always in a mood that will allow you to produce something you can feel positive about.

This does not have to be a problem. I often find that I am at my most creative at times when I am unable to sit down and write, such as at work or at a friend's house, and I suspect this is because in those moments I am not actively trying to create. That is the right time and the right place for me. Regardless of how frustrating it can be, in those moments I am in the correct mindset. You have to discover what your writing mindset is and when you are at your most creative.

There are many things that you can do to get into the writing 'mood'. Activities such as timed writing for five or ten minutes (no need to stop to think about what you are writing, just get on with it!) can whip up lots of ideas that were previously lost somewhere in the back of your brain. Reading or taking a walk can inspire you in ways that sitting at a desk facing a blank sheet of paper cannot. They can also give you a much needed break from writing.

Ideas do not always flow freely when you are putting pressure on yourself to create something. When you write and how you feel when you begin to write can make a huge difference on the result.

Laura Marie Clark

Write a Little Every Day

If we want to get or keep an athletic figure, then we need to exercise often. The same logic applies to writing. There is no right or wrong amount of time to spend writing each day: it all depends on what works for you. If you see yourself as a professional and want to make a career out of writing, then you'll have to spend more time doing it then someone who is doing it purely as a hobby.

Not only will you need more practice and more experience, you'll also need to be more aware of the best time of day for you to write and the kind of mood you need to be in to really involve yourself in your work. Even if you're only writing for fun, you should always try to do it a little bit every day so that you can keep those writing muscles active.

It can be something as simple as scribbling a haiku down on a piece of scrap paper or something as significant as getting a couple of chapters of a novel typed up on a computer. If you're busy, get out your pen and paper and jot down some notes whenever you get the chance. There's always a few minutes to write in the morning when you wake up, or at night before you go to bed. I often find myself typing rapidly on my phone after work, recording little bits of information, inspiration and verses that I've thought of throughout the day.

The point is that if you practice a little every day, you'll gradually build upon your writing skills and find yourself a stronger, more experienced writer.

Laura Marie Clark

Begin With What You Know

As writers, we always sound more confident when we have in depth knowledge of what we are discussing, whether we are writing an essay on religion, a love poem or a story about World War I. It may seem like an obvious point, but you may be surprised by the multitude of things you understand or have experienced that you can write about.

Are you or have you studied something that completely animates you? Teach me about it. Take that subject and show me your enthusiasm for it through your writing. As a reader, I am always more excited about poems and stories on subjects that I can tell the writer has a deep passion for.

Think about music or imagery that moves you. You can use something you've seen while you're out walking, like a beautiful sunset, or shopping, like a man begging for change on the street. Give me those heartwarming or heart wrenching moments on a page. The stronger you feel about it, the more likely you will be to get those feelings across in your writing and make me feel the same.

Where do you work? What are the everyday tasks that you do at work or home? The perspective that you have on everyday things can be very revealing, and I often find that it is easier to develop my characters when I do not have to research what they do. I already have a connection with them because I already understand their point of view. When you next experience the pressure or the passion of an everyday thing, use it to create something new.

Use the negatives as well as the positives. Our happiest moments can conjure up magnificent imagery and create wonderful imagery, but often it is our darkest moments that inspire the most powerful writing. Fears, nightmares and tragedies can be turned into incredibly moving work.

Within clouds of torment
Plagued by terror, haunting thoughts
Great strength I summon, pushing

At the walls of rigid depression
To climb the mountain of my mind

Remember that your mind contains ideas and images that nobody else's mind does. Your emotion.

Laura Marie Clark

Find Your Writing Space

You have the correct equipment for you to write effectively, but where do you like to be when you write? You need to find a place where you are comfortable throwing ideas around and can focus on your writing. This place varies from person to person and can also depend on what exactly you are writing. Is your poetry space the same as your novel space? Is your space for creating ideas the same as your writing space?

You will sometimes see people sitting on their own in coffee shops, busy writing in the middle of a crowded place. They might find inspiration in a passing stranger or a scene that they witness. Others feel more inspired by the natural world. They need quiet environments where there is nothing whatsoever to distract them. Others enjoy writing while they're in a library or traveling or listening to music.

Personally, I cannot work in a crowd or a public space. There's nothing better than sitting at my desk in my bedroom with a movie or TV show on as background noise (not loud enough for me to become distracted by the volume). At the end of the day, it is all about what you prefer: there's no such thing as the perfect place to sit down and write. The place where you feel inspired might not be the same place as the one in which you write successfully.

Laura Marie Clark

Writing Tools

Is there anyone out there an old fashioned writer still using pen and paper? I am one of the few who still does as I don't trust technology 100%. I am writing this article on my third laptop, sixth computer out of all I have owned, because devices like these are not meant to last very long. I have seen books older than me that are still in excellent condition. But there's nothing wrong with using a computer, laptop, tablet or phone to write, but I highly recommend you have back up of your work on an external hard drive and/or disc just in case your device gets stolen, lost or crashes.

My ultimate writing tools consist of a Dr. Grip pen (my favorite) and one of the many notebooks in every corner of my apartment. There's something magical when the ink flows smoothly on that fresh white paper, and the right pen is most important according to Natalie Goldberg in her book, Writing Down the Bones, where she explains "It should be a fast writing pen because your thoughts are always much faster than your hand" (5). You want the pen to feel comfortable in your hand and I prefer those with a larger body and grip with a smooth gel ink. These usually have re-fillable cartridges so you don't have to keep spending money on new pens.

I am definitely a notebook junkie, because every school supply season I end up buying 3 or 4 college-rule notebooks for my collection – and why not? They are much cheaper during that time anyway. And don't limit your selection; buy them in various sizes and colors to keep in your pocket or purse. A writer will often get thoughts at the most inopportune times, so we must always be prepared. I keep one in every room and even take them with me to a doctor's offices, at work to use during breaks, or anywhere else I know I will have a long wait. Writing in a notebook before bed also helps to calm my mind of those thoughts that usually keep me up at night.

One final thought – many of us who write often suffer with insomnia, as our brains are working overtime with all the ways we need to express ourselves. Using all these electronic devices are to blame as many studies show the lighting stimulates our minds making it harder to fall asleep. So the old fashion writing tools can have some advantage in this high tech world.

What are some of your favorite writing tools – old and new?

Donna J. Sanders

Writing Ideas

There is nothing worse for a writer than having absolutely nothing to write about. In order to avoid this, you should have a variety of writing ideas available to you at all times. These should be a range of things that you have previously envisioned but never expanded upon that you can delve into at the right moment. They can vary from genres to topics to characters and more.

A good way to ensure that you have plenty of ideas at your fingertips is to keep a writing notebook or journal. This can be used to jot down any writing ideas you have whenever they come to you, whether they are complicated plots or single word prompts that you can come back to later. Single sentences or lines of poetry are a great way to inspire you when you feel stuck, so write them down for use on a day when you struggle!

If you find it hard to generate writing ideas, there are many things you can do to get the inspiration flowing. Your idea does not have to be the most ingenious, inventive one in the world, nor does it have to be wholly unique (and let's face it, that would be a challenge). Reading is an easy source of ideas, as is looking for writing prompts.

You could also time yourself, taking five or ten minutes to write anything that comes to mind, then pick out the good ideas. You could brainstorm ideas on a piece of paper or post it notes (which allow you to move them around and connect them in more way that just a single sheet of paper). You could take ideas from movies or songs or posters you walk past on your day to work or school.

However you come up with your ideas, your notebook will be invaluable on those days when you feel uninspired: there will already be a list of ideas written down for you. All you will have to do is connect the dots.

Laura Marie Clark

Creativity Comes First

Spelling and good grammar are essential to good writing. If you make frequent mistakes in either of these areas, then your readers can become confused or distracted from your piece. They complete what you have written by supporting it and making it appear professional, but they do not necessarily make your writing good by themselves. A weak sentence is still a weak sentence whether the spelling and grammar are correct or not.

This is why creativity should come first when you are writing. You need to focus on the content of what you are writing when you begin, and not how it is laid out on the page. Later on, you can edit, change punctuation, check your spelling and replace or rewrite as you please. But in a first draft, these elements are not essential.

When you read through your draft, you will be more likely to spot these mistakes or changes in the mood of your writing. You will be able to tell the feeling of your writing and the places where words do not seem to work together, as well as where you could change the lengths of sentences or the punctuation within your sentences.

So the next time you sit down to write, let editing take a back seat! Your creativity is more important.

Laura Marie Clark

If It Doesn't Work, Move On

It isn't always easy to discontinue something you've been working on. As writers, we sometimes catch ourselves working on a piece that becomes worse and worse with every word we add. It happens to us all and it's incredibly disheartening when we realize that there's no other option but to give up. Whether our writing is confused, maddeningly vague or completely lost, we don't always want to do that. We need to learn to challenge ourselves whilst also recognizing when something has beaten us.

I'm not suggesting that we should abandon our ideas entirely on these occasions. During Writing 201, a poetry course by The Daily Post, I wrote many attempts at poetry that were ripped from my notebook, screwed up into a ball and tossed under my desk in frustration. More often than not, however, some element of that original idea made it into the final poem. There had been a creative spark in that first version that eventually came out.

So if there's a line, a character or even an overlying theme that you love, you can still salvage it. Scrap the failing piece and begin again from line one. The ability to distinguish between something that is working and something that isn't working is important for every writer.

Laura Marie Clark

Dare To Put Yourself Out There

There is something I must admit to. As a teenager, I posted a poem I was very pleased with on a popular website that's viewed by a massive number of writers and readers each day (I don't remember the name of it, only that I avoided it for a long time until I forgot about it). Distraught by the inconsiderate and tactless criticism of someone I would never meet, I quickly deleted it. I crawled back into the private den where I hid the rest of my writing for the following few years until I became bold enough to try again.

Whatever you do, don't be me. Oh, the criticism taught me a thing or two about my own writing and where I was going wrong, but I took it badly and responded to it poorly. Cruel criticism is unnecessary, but as writers posting in a world where so many can remain anonymous, we must not be afraid of it. The best readers will offer constructive criticism when it is needed, designed to help us rather than humiliate us.

In order to improve, we must be ready to face the negative feedback along with the positive. Perhaps our paragraphs need to be broken up. Perhaps the layout of our poem distracts the reader from the message we intend to convey. Perhaps our vocabulary is unsuited to the genre of our piece. Perhaps we could have emphasized our statements with the choice of alternative punctuation. Whatever it is, we can only learn if we are told.

Laura Marie Clark

Writing For Personal Fulfillment

This is something that most of us do at some point. For some of us, writing is about more than simply personal pursuits – it is a professional endeavor, concerned with continuous development and regular submissions. Those who are more focused on personal fulfillment when writing may also hope to achieve these things, though with a more relaxed time span.

Writing for personal fulfillment is a great exercise for everyone. It can help us to heal personal wounds, whether we write a first person account of our experiences or choose to fictionalize them. Not only does it allow us to let off some proverbial steam, it also challenges us when we're writing. Recording personal accounts is an excellent test of our skills as a writer as we have to put our own opinions and feelings into words.

No matter how difficult it may be to write about ourselves, the complexities of explaining ourselves and turning ourselves into a character on a page is incredibly rewarding. The more that we write, the more fulfillment we can get out of it. We do not always have to use a touching subject when we are writing about ourselves, either. You can write down your opinions on politics or education or whatever else takes your fancy. You can make a list of things you like and dislike. Whatever you write about when you aim for personal fulfillment, you will find it a way to challenge yourself. You may even find yourself expanding upon your beliefs to further understand yourself.

Laura Marie Clark

What Should I Write About?

"You're going to write about that? But that's topic's been done to death!" This can be a problematic thing for a writer to hear. There are always common topics that we want to write about, and the fact that they are common should not sway us from writing about them. Our natural instinct is to write about something that we are familiar with, even if the subject has been tackled again and again by many different writers. What is going to make your poem (or story) unique?

Of course, you are going to write about something that you feel is important enough to be said. Can you write about it from an unusual or new perspective? You don't have to be a pioneer of a new way of thinking. Great poems stick with people because the language and imagery within them is special: it has touched them in a way that other poems on the same topic have not.

Let's use "love" as an example. Many people write love poetry (or discuss the topic of love).

Most of us, if not all of us, have a go at it. Writers are all moved by someone at some point, but how do you say something new about a topic that has been on people's mind for thousands of years? That's the thing you need to think about when you're creating poetry. Allow for expression so that you can touch your readers with your words. Try to avoid a string of clichés and think about what could give a fresh perspective to this subject. This is the trick of poetry. It's not easy to think of new ways to look at old subjects, but when you do think of something that sound original, you will write some great poetry that will stick in your readers' minds.

Laura Marie Clark

Engage With Others In Your Position

When we post something and come back a few hours later to discover not a single view or like, it can be very discouraging.
A multitude of questions can attack us at once.

- What did I do wrong?
- Why don't people like my post?
- How can I get more people to view my writing?
- Should I have posted something else?
- Am I a bad writer?

The answer to the final question is no. I do not believe in "bad" writers, I believe in writers who are still developing their technique. The other four questions are not as easy to answer. You may be creating top quality material, but if nobody is viewing it then you can still feel dejected.

One thing that can help us, not only in terms of getting more page views or likes but also to become more confident writers, is to engage with other people who are in the same position. By exploring, reading and commenting we can gain ideas, an insight into popular topics or blogs, and helpful, positive advice on where we might be able to improve. Reading the work of published authors will always be good for writers, but reading what our peers have created can teach us a great deal about our own writing, too.

Go to a blog you particularly enjoy. Read through their posts and pick out two: one you really like and one that you don't. Think about the things that work well in the first post and those that don't work in the second. The next time you write, keep these things in mind and see whether they apply to your own writing. It could give you some helpful hints on what makes a great piece.

Laura Marie Clark

Staying Motivated

The New Year approaches and some have probably set their goals to write more, to get published, to step outside of their bubble and finally share their creations with the world; all admirable goals. Some will start writing and can't stop. Some will write until their minds are empty. Others will hit stumbling blocks, maybe even get frustrated and quit. I cringe at the latter because there is always something to write about.

In these hard economic times, where people are becoming more and more selfish; instead of getting too frustrated, depressed, or extending a negative attitude to rude people – put those intense emotions on paper. Just free write or turn it into something poetic and you will find that it can also be great therapy. If you find yourself in a place where you see the strangest of things or people, write a humorous or mysterious poem about your observations. If something in nature you never noticed before captures your eye, give a description or write about how it made you feel in that very moment. Use your surroundings and your everyday schedule to find material to write.

Many social media and blog sites have writing prompts every day. Scour some pages or use the hashtag #writingprompt to find them. Some will even have writing challenges for a particular month that many will participate in, and some sites may even share your work. Take advantage of these opportunities to get your poetry seen.

Get prepared for National Poetry Month in April. I had three of my poems featured on Good Magazine and Maria Shriver's blog last year by using their special hashtags on twitter when I posted my poems. Many other sites are looking for artists to promote Poetry Month, so keep a handful of poems to post every day and pay attention to the hashtags everyone else is using.

If words are not stimulating your mind, picture prompts are another alternative. Some sites use this to motivate as well. If you can't find a prompt, use Google to find a theme or subject you want to write about. You can search by type: photo, drawing, painting, color or black and white. If nothing on the Internet appeals to you, browse some of your own photos or photos from a friend's page for some inspiration.

Writing Tips - Volume 1

Try writing a poem from this photo I took at the zoo and leave it in the comments. I just happened to capture this shot while the tiger was playing with another one, and resting for a moment. Do his eyes tell a story? What is he feeling after that playful romp? You could even write from the perspective of the tiger as he sees me with the camera. Have fun with it!

And keep finding other ways to stay motivated to write in 2016!

Donna J. Sanders

Stuck? Try Something New

Stuck? Try Something New

There will always be those moments when you feel the oncoming doom associated with – gasp – writer's block, but there are ways to overcome it. One of the ways to get your brain working and restart your writing is to look at something you have not previously (or recently) attempted.

This could be a different point of view. If you usually write from a woman's point of view, try a man's instead; if you usually write from a rich person's point of view, try a poor person's opinion; or a homeless person's; or a dog's, and so on. You do not necessarily have to write something new: you can use something you have previously written and look at it from the opinion of another character or an onlooker. This will force you to look at a situation in a new way and produce a different outcome. Another method is trying to write in a new genre. There are always more genres for you to explore, whether romance or horror or science fiction or non-fiction. Producing something in an area that is completely new to you will encourage you to think about your writing and the language you use in an alternate way.

You could also discover a new talent within a genre you had never considered writing in before. If a new genre is too much, try a new topic within your favorite genre. For example, if you write romance, try writing about young love instead of a breakup. You could also try a new style of writing. In poetry, you could use a form of poetry that you do not often use. Those who usually write without any specific form can benefit from adhering to stricter rules, and vice versa. In stories, you can try to write in a different way – such as more or less dialogue, or longer or shorter sentences.

Laura Marie Clark

Take Advantage of Prompts

Whether it's from a writing course, a dedicated prompt blog or a new blog trying to establish itself, writers who are looking for inspiration should search for prompts that capture their attention and get their brain working like mad. If a prompt doesn't fill you with writing ideas, then there are plenty of others out there that will.

Different types of prompts work better for different writers. If words work better for you, focus on single word prompts. Prompts like 'right', 'love' and 'travel' can be interpreted in so many ways that it is always interesting to discover what people have created from such a simple cue. If sentences get your mind going, then there are blogs out there to suit you, too. If whole paragraphs are your thing, then don't worry – you're covered as well. If pictures inspire you the most, then there are dedicated places for you to find prompts and inspiration. Or, pick a mixture and experiment to see what you can create.

When you write for a prompt, you're combining your creative ideas with information that you might not have thought of on your own. It might not be something that you would usually write about, but in exploring new ways to write and new subjects to write about, you're challenging yourself and expanding your horizons. If there's a word count or a specific form to use, then you're really challenging yourself. Producing something you're pleased with in answer to a prompt can be incredibly rewarding for a writer.

Furthermore, if you're interested in being published, find an indie publisher in your genre that posts prompts or writing ideas on social media. By discovering what they're looking for and filling in their prompts, you can get your writing judged and review yourself on a professional level.

Laura Marie Clark

Music as Inspiration

When you sit down to write and the ADD kicks in or a million distractions prevent you from finishing one sentence, it means time to find a new angle. If you don't have the luxury of finding that solitude in nature where the noise of civilization is miles away, then may I suggest the next best thing – MUSIC. I find my creativity flowing more when I listen to music. For me, classical movie scores do the trick and I pick and choose which I want to listen to depending on the topic I am writing.

My playlist includes many Science Fiction/Fantasy movie scores as they are my favorite kind to watch.

When I feel nostalgic and want to write about my past or the happenings of the world, I like the soundtracks of apocalyptic movies like "Oblivion," "Divergent" and "The Time Machine." The music can take me to the past and future often inspiring poems of the way I want to change myself or the world. When I feel like writing something quirky or adventurous, I play "Pirates of the Caribbean," "Alice in Wonderland" or "Prince of Persia" soundtracks. When I want nature to inspire me "Avatar" is my soundtrack of choice. And for those times when I feel like I am on top of the world "Man of Steel" or the "X-Men: First Class" scores liven me up to write with positivity.

The same way these movies and books in the same genre take me away far from reality, the music becomes my escape. Headphones are a wonderful tool – use them! You will be able to block out those annoying patrons whispering at the library or maybe your husband sitting on the couch blasting the television when he plays video games. Music has helped me focus and even inspire my writing as I play out certain fantasies in my head. I don't know how I would write without it.

Donna J. Sanders

Observing People

She inserted a new piercing into her body whenever she felt an internal pain. Some were a memorial to the ones she lost, while others were to mask her own agony. She would touch them and sometimes pick at them as if to remind her who they were for. Maybe she felt that if she put more holes in her soul, the pain would eventually seep out.

This description is not about me but observations of someone encountered in my life. Not to insult her or demean her methods, but to delve deeper into how she coped with the demons she was fighting. I ended up writing a poem about her, posted it on social media, and it received great feedback. So many others could relate to the poem, as it was similar to the way they dealt with pain, and some were surprised to find out it was not about me.

I am not always my poems.

There's absolutely nothing wrong with writing poems about our own lives, but from tapping into memories of those who have passed us by or observing a stranger on the street, we can capture another unique soul and put a moment of their lives into words. Life is full of so many interesting people waiting to be poetry.

Make it a habit to notice behaviors in a waiting room, or recall a conversation from the chatty cashier at the grocery store, and maybe even observe a few people at a park or mall. We encounter people every day and there has to be a few who we find fascinating or leave us more curious than before.

Edna St. Vincent Millay included some very detailed observations in her poem "Portrait By a Neighbor." From the title of the poem, with the use of "by" rather than "of," it is unclear if the author speaks of herself or an actual neighbor. She leaves the poem open to interpretation, but her description is quite precise and paints an interesting portrait of a woman just doing her chores.

Like many poets who use nature as their muse, people we don't even know can be used the same way. Pay more attention to a co-worker, a cab driver, or a neighbor as Millay did and it could possibly yield an amazing poem. Use the gift of observation to get those creative juices flowing when you have exhausted writing about yourself.

Donna J. Sanders

Using Words

Writing prompts and inspirational calls are great incentives to get your creative juices flowing, but sometimes a simple word or phrase can inspire me to write. Being the book nerd that I am, I often follow or subscribe to "word of the day" pages and sites where an unusual word or phrase will appear and a great poem will come of it.

On Instagram I follow @whiskeybooks – found by reading another poets post. They often post a word or phrase with its meaning. One in particular which I never heard of – L'appel du Vide – a French phrase meaning: call of the void, and often used to describe the urge to jump from high places. I loved the phrase so much and was determined to use it in a poem. I read its meaning over and over again and then thought of the Grand Canyon to be my subject. I ended up writing one of my favorite poems out of the thousands I have written by using this beautiful foreign phrase:

L'appel du Vide

How can one not be in awe

where Earth meets heaven

a fortress of plateaus

glistening in many a majestic sunrise

canyons carved by rivers of rage

gouged by nature's distress

I would be humbled in its presence

overwhelmed by its power

anxiously waiting for it

to swallow me whole

As writers, we have the ability to see beauty in words – whether they reflect negative aspects (e.g., rage, prison, thorns) – a good writer can manipulate such words to create sensuous images or use them symbolically. So sign up on all your social media sites and search for pages like: Words of Inspiration, Inspirational Quotes, even the Dictionary will send you a word of the day on their app or via email. Snatch a word or two to use the next time you need inspiration. And always take a moment to see what pages inspire other artists as well.

Donna J. Sanders

Listen With Everything

We all have varying taste in music. Some like a more energetic tune to get their day started, others prefer something soothing. When I was in high school, I had to have rock music blaring while I did my homework. As a young adult, I loved trance and techno, especially when doing chores around the house. Today, anything with a violin can put my heart in a trance. The world could stop and nothing would matter, as long as I hear the melodic sounds of my favorite instrument.

When I started to write more and more, I learned to listen to music more carefully. By taking a moment to pause and just listen to the way it made me feel, inspiration would naturally flow. But I don't always need music to write. Often I will sit in silence and listen to the subtle noises coming from outside my window; from the soft drizzle of rain on a stormy day, to the planes flying overhead. At the beach, the sounds of the crashing waves or the hum of a boat engine can be innovative.

But don't limit listening to just the ears; use the entire body. Use your eyes to watch as the breeze let the leaves rustle and write where the travels may take them. When you go outside and hear your neighbor shoveling his driveway, how does it feel when that first flake of snow touches your skin? If you adore your cat's purr, what emotions fill you from the texture of her fur? Focus on all the other senses as you listen.

Try a few listening exercises and see what the results may be:

- Spend a few minutes sitting in your car and listen to the sounds with the windows down, look at the floor mats or console and observe what objects are laying around, and close your eyes and feel the textures of the seats and the steering wheel. Then write.

- If you are in a restaurant, observe the sounds coming from the kitchen or the tables next to you, the smells of the food carried by the waiter walking by, and the unusual items from the restaurants interior theme. Write about your experience there by tapping into these observations.

- You can even listen when reading. Pick a short story, a poem or a few pages from a book, and spend a few moments putting yourself in the scene or how you think the poet would sound when reciting the emotions written. Close the book, take a few moments to recall what you read and then write a response to the text.

A hearing impaired person can still feel the vibrations of sound and it is how they are able to listen. They also rely on closed caption text when watching television, and must observe an actor's expression to captivate the emotions we usually hear in the tone of a voice. Listening is something we often take for granted and don't appreciate until we start to lose it as we get older. So take advantage of listening well; as writers, we should be able to do it better than most.

Donna J. Sanders

Sources: Goldberg, Natalie. Writing Down the Bones. Boston: Shambhala, 2005. Print (59)

Expand Your Vocabulary ... But Don't Overuse Long or Obscure Words

Do you sometimes find yourself looking back at what you've written only to discover that you've repeated the same word or phrase in your sentence or paragraph? It can be hard to find an appropriate replacement word on these occasions. As writers, we all have words that we avoid using for fear of overuse. We would be wise to locate words with similar meanings to add to our vocabulary, as repetitive writing can cause us to lose the interest of our readers.

Yet this should be done with caution. I have several friends whose writing too often demonstrates how academically minded they are by making their reader feel stupid. Every other sentence will contain a word that I'll have to look up in a dictionary and I often feel distracted from the original purpose of the piece (which is to be read). Their writing style confuses the reader. Nothing flows. The meaning is forgotten. Too many long or uncommon words can be just as bad as repeating words again and again.

Let's look at an example using the first paragraph:
 Do you intermittently discern yourself scrutinizing what you've authored to ascertain that you've replicated the same word or parlance in your clause or passage? It can be vexing to provide a felicitous surrogate word during these occurrences. As writers, we aggregate words that we obviate for presentiment of overuse…

Okay, I'm being silly now, but I think you get the picture.
 It's important to find some middle ground between plain and complicated language. If you're using some common words too often, think carefully about the word you need to replace and whether your new word is suitable there. Discovering new words and using them appropriately can improve the standard of our writing, but it can also send out the wrong message.

Laura Marie Clark

There Are Great Characters Out There (In The Real World)

We have all seen people who have made us curious. How many times have you looked at someone and wondered what makes them tick? Their life story, their interests, the events that have led them to be where they are now … there are countless things that interest us about people we do not know. When we build up stories about other people from the bits of information that we might have, we are creating a character of our own.

Another way in which strangers can inspire us is through their actions and small snippets of conversation that we hear between them. People can say things that make us laugh and wonder what discussion they might be involved in. Can you fit these words into a story or use them as the central theme of a poem? Can you consider why that individual might be acting in the way they are? It could be something silly, like a bee that they are trying to get away from, or something more serious and personal that deeply affects their character.

Creating memorable characters is central to building stories that people can identify with and find interesting, but there is no need to begin them from scratch. There are endless amounts of people out there who you can use to create striking and realistic individuals to include in your writing.

Laura Marie Clark

Use The Unusual Details

Hawaii is a place of natural wonders; with vibrant plumeria trees on every corner, beaches with black sands and brilliant blue waters, and volcanic scenery that looks like another world. But these descriptions are nothing new. They can be seen on any Internet photo search. How to truly describe the island one has to depict the culture and flavors experienced: the taste and smells, the encounters with residents, and even the most unusual events.

I got married on the island of Maui at sunrise and it was NOT the picture perfect wedding. It rained so heavily the day before, tons of red dirt from the hills rolled onto the main roads and the ground was too saturated at the location we originally picked to get married. While looking at our video of the ceremony, we noticed a tourist boogie boarding on the beach, with the waves wiping him out several times. During the photographer session, the hotel sprinklers turned on by the ledge we were using. Everything didn't go as planned in this paradise, but it made the moments memorable.

When you want to describe a place you visit, leave out the obvious. Tap into the senses and go beyond the scenery. If you are walking through a market, what are the aromas of food, perfumes, or even the fabrics hanging on a rack? If you are on the beach, depict the textures of unusual items you find in the sand. If the cruise schedule didn't go as planned because of bad weather, relay how you occupied the time and what you observed of others on the ship. It is the unusual details that will capture an audience.

Author Derek Walcott uses literary magic to describe the island of St. Lucia in his epic, Omeros. In the excerpt (pictured right), he portrays Christmas time by the smells that travel with the wind: the scent of the asphalt after being drizzled with rain, the sizzle of a morning fish fry, inhaling the aroma of spiced ham, but also the hint of a foreboding death. Walcott uses this method throughout the book and his specific descriptions feed the reader with the rich culture of the island, making it easier to enjoy the lengthy poem.

In the chapter "Writing About Place: The Travel Article," William Zinsser says: Find details that are significant. They may be important to your narrative; they may be unusual, or colorful, or comic, or entertaining. But make sure they do useful work. -Zissner, On Writing Well

Zissner explains further to stay away from cliché descriptions. Even though a popular vacation spot may have been written about over and over again, he challenges the reader to make it his/her own by seeing it from a different perspective and using one's own unique experiences.

Donna J. Sanders

Sources: Walcott, Derek. Omeros. New York: Noonday Press, 1995. 223. Print

Zinsser, William. On Writing Well. New York: Collins, 2006. 116-131. Print

Creating Strong Emotions

Life is incomplete without emotions. The same applies to your writing, and particularly to your poetry. You do not have to get yourself worked up into an emotional state in order to create emotion within your writing. Most of us know the feeling of being in love with someone or something, or the sadness of losing someone or something that we care about deeply. As a writer, these emotions are powerful tools that you can use in order to create a strong impression on your audience. We have all read poetry and fiction that has moved us in some way. When you read something that greatly affects you, consider why it makes you feel that way.

Ask yourself the following questions:

- How does the language shape your emotions?

- What sort of imagery does it evoke?

- Look at the words the writers use and think about how they have shaped their piece: are there strong metaphors? Short lines? Effective words?

- Does the poem remind you of something that has happened to you personally, a story you've seen in the news, or something else?

You will probably find that the writer has not mentioned the specific emotion they wish to evoke by name. Rather than telling you how they or their subject feels, they have shown you how they feel, making you more involved in their piece. This is a key skill when you are writing about emotions. If someone is angry or upset, instead of saying how they feel, you can use destructive imagery, such as a natural disaster. If someone is happy or excited, you can use positive imagery, such as warm weather and a calm environment. This way, you can inject more effective emotions into your writing.

Laura Marie Clark

Be A Witness

We are all witnesses. Some of our lives may not be all that dramatic, but we have stories to tell of the things we have seen and heard. Poets not only delve deep into their souls and write about the madness that keeps them sane, but they can also use the senses to make an audience aware of particular moments. Poets can also be historians by recording trivial times and important events into their work.

With unlimited access to current events in the world, poets have the ability to express their point of view on social issues, as poets like Langston Hughes and Pablo Neruda did in their time. Hughes, a social activist as well, wrote about life from his point of view as a black man in America. Neruda, heavily involved in the politics of his country, Chile, not only wrote about love but the desire for social change as wars were brewing.

Poets can also write from personal events. Our experiences with domestic abuse, divorce, being in a foster home, being bullied at school, losing a job or a death in the family, can not only be therapeutic to write about but record times in our life we want to forget. However, revisiting those moments and sharing them with the world can help another soul who is dealing with a similar issue and not know how to cope. To show them how you were able to move on and strive, can possibly change another's life. That is the power of poetry.

I always advise poets to keep a journal or notebook everywhere: on a nightstand, in your car, at your desk and even in your purse or pocket. We witness everyday while following our daily routines, and you never know when something you see or hear will be significant enough to inspire you to write.

Donna J. Sanders

Leave Your Most Powerful Image For Last

Whether you are writing poetry or a story, you are inevitably going to be building up to something – a grand finale. Whether that is some catastrophic events that causes mass devastation or the recognition of the beauty of something completely ordinary and every day, your ending is key to your readers understanding. It summarizes everything you have written, whether you round it off nicely or finish with a cliff-hanger.

Your readers are more likely to remember a strong piece of writing with an emotive or powerful ending than something that seems to fade away. Mastering how to end your piece is as important as discovering the best way to begin it: the end should have an impact or make a statement that resonates in your readers' minds.

There is no need to have an answer for everything you have written about. You can leave your writing as open to interpretation as you wish. Instead of trying everything in a neat knot, focus on finishing your piece with an image that will remain with your readers for the rest of the day. Every paragraph, chapter, verse or line is a step towards your ending. Build up the imagery that you use as you write, and end with the most powerful image you can.

Laura Marie Clark

Grammar

Colon and Semicolon

Colons (:) and semicolons (;) are punctuation marks that can help you to write English more effectively. They have very different uses that can easily become confused, and usually replace commas or full stops to change the way that you read a passage. Let's look at their different uses.

The Colon

The colon (:) introduces extra information that is related to the first statement. It can be used to introduce a list of items, such as a list of ingredients for a recipe. It can also be used to introduce an explanation or a conclusion by highlighting the second statement and showing that it logically follows the first. This means that you can use it to connect two sentences together in the place of a full stop if the second sentence further explains or concludes a statement made in the first.

The Semicolon

The semicolon (;) represents a break in a sentence that is stronger than a comma. It allows the writer to avoid overusing the comma. It can be used to separate items in a list when one or more of the items contain a comma (such as: Mr Smith, Mathematics; Mrs Jones, English; Mr Brown, Science …). It can also be used to link two sentences that are closely related to one another together. For example, you could use it to replace words such as 'and' and 'but' in a sentence.

These are some simple ways to use the colon and the semicolon in your writing. Learn how and when to use them to expand your knowledge of punctuation and improve your writing.

Laura Marie Clark

Too and To (and Two)

Here are some very simple words that are also very easy to get confused with one another. It's often difficult to spot these errors when you are editing, as all of these words are so small and similar. We'll start with the easiest word: two (and in the number 2). That spelling should be the easiest for you to remember when you're writing. The other two (too and to, that is) get confused more often, especially by new writers. They mean very different things and if you do not get them the right way around, it can confuse your readers. Let's take a look.

Too

This can mean the same as 'also'. For example: Mary has an ice cream. John has one, too. It can also mean 'extra'. Use too when there is an increase in something, for example an increase in size (too large), temperature (too hot) or speed (too fast). This usage emphasizes the word (large, hot and fast) For example: Mary's feet were too large for her shoes. John's music was too loud and it woke his parents.

To

This is a preposition. In this case, to always precedes a noun. Use it when expressing a direction, place or position. For example: Mary went to Italy. John went to Blackpool. It can also be used with the infinitive form of verbs. An infinitive verb is the basic version of the verb (how it appears in the dictionary). Infinitives can be complicated. Here are some simple examples: Mary needs to study. John wants to help.

There are many websites dedicated to explaining the differences between too and to where you can learn more about infinitives and read other examples. Remembering when to use each of these words will improve your grammar and your writing.

Laura Marie Clark

It's vs. Its

I have had a lot of trouble with it's and its in the past, and I'm certainly not the only one. These two little words can leave many writers, especially beginners, scratching their heads. When exactly do you use "it's", and when do you use "its"?

This was a problem for me for a long time. At some point during school, I'm sure my English teacher must have taught me this grammar rule, and yet all I remember are big red arrows pointing to unnecessary or non-existent apostrophes. I didn't properly learn how to tell when to use "it's" and when to use "its" until a couple of years ago, when the rule suddenly clicked into place.

The rule is quite simple. "It's" is a contraction. This means that it is the shortening of two words (in this case, "it is") into one word. You can use it place of "it is", "she is". "he is" or "that is". "Its" is a possessive pronoun. Use it in place of "his" or "her". An easier way to understand the difference between "it's" and "its" is to look at some examples. Let's do that now.

Example of it's

"That's Mary's dog. It's crazy. It's always chasing people."
In this example, "it's" is a contraction. You can tell because you could rewrite the sentence like this:
"That's Mary's dog. It is (she is, he is) crazy. It is (she is, he is) always chasing people."

Example of its

"Steven's dog is always chasing its tail."
In this example, "its" is a possessive. You cannot say Steven's dog is always chasing it is tail", which is why you do not use an apostrophe. You could rewrite the sentence like this, though: "Steven's dog is always chasing her tail."

Laura Marie Clark

There, They're and Their

A common mistake many writers make is to confuse there, they're and their. It is all too easy to do. Though they sound the same when spoken, the meaning of each of these words is very different. In this tip, I will remind you when to use each of these words in order to improve your writing.

There Example 1:

"There once was a man from Kentucky …"
In this example, the writer has used 'there' to talk about a place, Kentucky.

Example 2:

"Look Fred, there is a puppy here!"
In this example, the writer has used 'there' with a 'to be' verb (be, is, am, are, was, were). It indicates the existence of the puppy.

They're Example:

"They're bad kids. Don't play with them."
In this example, the writer has used 'they're' to discuss a subject, the kids. Remember that 'they're' is actually two words: 'they' and 'are'.

Their Example:

"Anne and Sarah shared their chocolates with their friends."
In this example, the writer has used 'their' to indicate possession. The chocolates belong to Anne and Sarah, and the friends are linked to them.

Laura Marie Clark

Adverbs

If you're taking part in Blogging U's Writing 101 challenge at the moment, or you've taken part in the past, you should be aware of how many adverbs you use when you write. One of the more recent posts asked bloggers to write a description of something or someone they had seen without using any adverbs. Many people, including myself, found it an enlightening exercise that revealed how often we rely on adverbs.

Adverbs are words that add further description to a verb, adjective or other adverb. They give further information, such as to explain how an action is performed. Most of them end in -ly, such as quickly, slowly and carelessly. Though they can provide us with extra information, they are not powerful words. You do not need to remove them from everything you write, but it's good to be aware of how often you use them.

Let's take a look at some examples of adverbs and alternative sentences without adverbs:

1. He sat lazily in the armchair.
He slouched in the armchair.

2. They shouted loudly at the passing car.
They roared at the passing car.

3. The book was balanced carefully on the edge of the shelf.
The book was perched on the edge of the shelf.

In each of these examples, the adverb has been removed and the verb (sat, shouted, balanced) has been replaced by a stronger word that emphasizes the action. Have a look at the adverbs you use in your own writing and see if you can do the same thing.

Laura Marie Clark

Watch Your Tenses

We often change tenses unconsciously when we're speaking. We can switch from one to another with ease in a conversation, and the tense change doesn't matter. It therefore isn't uncommon for us to also move between tenses when we're writing, although it's more important if we want to maintain the flow of our work. It can be frustrating to see that something we have started to write includes a combination of tenses, which can throw the audience off the focus of our piece.

Let's look at an example:

Sheila reached up and took the large book from the shelf, then flicked it open and began to read. Her fingers followed the text across the page, her whole face a picture of concentration. The story is captivating and she longs to share it with all of her friends.

As you can see, the final sentence is in the present tense, rather than in past tense like the rest of the paragraph. This is something you can to avoid when you're writing. A good way to do this is to decide on a tense before you start writing. If you find yourself moving between tenses often, you will need to focus on being consistent. Practice by writing a few short stories in various tenses to ensure you are maintaining the same tense throughout.

Laura Marie Clark

Writing Tips - Volume 1

Metaphor and Simile

Metaphor and Simile are great devices that you can use to create powerful imagery in your poetry. They can both provide a form of comparison between two things and can add suggestion to your writing. They are basic but important tools for you to master.

What is a metaphor?

A metaphor is a sentence (or phrase) that says one thing is actually something else.

Here's an example: "Her eyes are diamonds."

We know that her eyes are not actually diamonds, but the metaphor implies that they share similar qualities. You might think of orbs that shimmer, precious gems, or eyes held as sacred by the writer. The suggestion is that they are to be remembered and stand out, demonstrating their importance. Most importantly, the metaphor provides a strong image of a beautiful pair of eyes.

What is a simile?

A simile is a sentence (or phrase) that says one thing is like something else.

Here's an example: "He was as fast as a cheetah." or "He was fast, like a cheetah."

The simile provides the man with the characteristics of a cheetah, suggesting that he is very quick or quicker than everyone else. It is not as abstract as a metaphor can be.

You should use a combination of metaphor and simile to create imagery in your poetry.

Laura Marie Clark

Alliteration

Alliteration is an important poetic technique to master. It can provide you with a noticeable, repetitive sound within your writing that adds to the rhythm.

What is Alliteration?

Alliteration is a technique where the beginning sounds of words repeat. This means that you do not have to repeat the same letters as long as there is the same sound at the beginnings of the words. For example, "cat" and "kettle" both have the same sound at the beginning, despite starting with different letters. A more complicated form of alliteration can be made by repeating the first syllables of the words.

When you are creating a piece with alliteration, you do not have to use the same sound at the beginning of every single word. There are also no rules of how much alliteration you should use: a good technique when writing alliteration is to read it back to yourself. If you cannot spot the alliteration, then your readers will probably not be able to spot it either.

Laura Marie Clark

Assonance

Assonance is a device primarily used in poetry. It adds an internal rhyme to the poem that allows the writer to create rhythm and can enhance the enjoyment of reading the piece. It can also be used to develop a 'mood' in the poem and enhance an emotion within your writing. Assonance can be very subtle, which is why it can develop a feeling within your work without the reader noticing it or becoming distracted by your use of this device.

What is Assonance?

Assonance occurs when the same vowel sound is used in two words that are close together. The words start with different consonant sounds. Remember that this does not necessarily mean you need to use the same vowels – you need to use the same vowel sounds. For instance, "may" and "weigh" use the same sound, but are created with different vowels.

Examples of Assonance:

"If I bleat when I speak it's because I just got . . . fleeced." – Al Swearengen
"The crumbling thunder of seas" – Robert Louis Stevenson
"I must confess that in my quest I felt depressed and restless." – Thin Lizzy

Laura Marie Clark

Vary the Lengths of Your Sentences

Some people only use short sentences. They don't say much in them. It makes their writing sound bland. Don't you hate that? You get bored of reading it. They don't seem to be able to change. Do they even know what a comma is?

Some people only use long sentences, the kind of sentences that you read and you wonder whether you'll ever be allowed to take a breath again because the sentence just keeps going on and on and on. Their sentences are long enough to take up an entire paragraph, and although they could break them up into smaller sentences that would make easier mouthfuls, for some reason they just keep going and going, as though the longer their sentences are the better their writing will be.

Obviously, you want to include sentences of various lengths if you want to keep your readers' attention. Short, sharp sentences can create tension. They can keep the audience on their toes if they're used at the right time. Long sentences can present details or lists or break up dialogue. The more that you write, the easier you will find it to recognize when you need to use a long or a short sentence.

If you find yourself using long or short sentences too often, think about where you could add or remove punctuation to vary the lengths of those sentences. A good exercise is to go back to something you have previously written and change the length of the sentences within that piece of writing. This way, you can see the effect that different sized sentences have on your words and the way that someone will read your writing.

Once you understand where to use long, medium and short sentences, you'll find you can have a more dramatic impact on your readers when you wish.

Laura Marie Clark

Onomatopoeia

When I say onomatopoeia, you might think of words like crash, woof or shout. These are all great examples of onomatopoeia. A large numbers of words in the English language are onomatopoeic words, and they can be useful to create the effect of sound within your writing.

What is Onomatopoeia?

Onomatopoeia is any word that means nothing more than the sound it makes. For instance, the word baa is an onomatopoeia, because baa is a sound. We recognize it and we all know what it sounds like. Many onomatopoeic words can also mean other things, usually related to their sound effect. The word crash, for example, can also be used to describe a moment when two things collide with one another.

Examples of Onomatopoeia:

There are many examples of onomatopoeia. Animal sounds are good examples. Words relating to speech, such as whisper or yell, are also onomatopoeia.

Using Onomatopoeia in your Writing:

There are many common onomatopoeic words in English. You do not need to avoid using them, but you should be careful not to overuse them in any one piece of writing. Try to find more obscure words with similar meanings and use them at strategic points when you want to create a dramatic pause or a powerful impact upon your reader.

Laura Marie Clark

Think Small . . . Write Big

Think Small...Write Big

Last week I stumbled across a magnificent picture of the galaxy above the plains of Africa with Mt Kilimanjaro in the distance. No city lights. No human presence. It was nature in all of its spectacular glory. If the picture took my breath away, I can only imagine what it must be like to see such a sight in person. To stand beneath those billions of stars while the vast jungle stirs, and being watched by one of the tallest volcanoes in the world. I would be a small girl in a very big world, surrounded by an even bigger universe. I stared at the picture for a long time and wrote until I ran out of ideas.

We look up to the stars, always wondering what may be out there, and the writers of many science fiction novels and movies have given us an abundance of possibilities. The galaxy is still a place beyond our comprehension that we may never fully explore. But what about some of the places you have been, or wish to see if it were possible? The Earth is large enough as it is, with many majestic places easily accessible.

Think about that moment when you first saw the Grand Canyon. Where were you standing and what could you see from that position? How long would it take to see the entire canyon? Imagine being lost where the river flows beneath, or the sounds you hear after the sun goes down. The canyon is such a colossal place, think about the tales you could tell from the mysteries and conspiracies that lie within.

How about the Great Wall of China? Have you ever stepped upon the stone and bricks that make up this giant fort? Imagine the journey one can take and the sights seen along the way. Take yourself back to the Ming Dynasty and picture what the construction site looked like. Think of the lives lost during its creation. Visualize what it must take to maintain the wall as it crumbles with age.

Often I will revisit photos I took from my trip to Maui. The island is such an amazing place, with quite a few diverse landscapes. One side of the island flows with lush foliage, fields of pineapple and sugar cane, and high surfing waves; while the other is barren, with a rocky coastline and black sand beaches. Driving to the top of the Haleakala volcano, it becomes another world. I understood why many describe it like the surface of Mars. With crimson soil, scattered cinder cones and the silversword plant (native only to Haleakala), spending a few hours here will leave you speechless. You really do feel the power of the mountain when you are standing on it.

Some of us don't have the luxury of traveling to such exotic places. We have to rely on photos to be inspired by the natural wonders of this world. So why not use our imagination to put ourselves into places we might not get to visit in our lifetime. Do some research on a place you wish to see: its construction or creation, the battles fought or the native people from the land, and what secrets are kept about this place? If you can't picture yourself there, write from the perspective of a bird flying above, or a river as it flows through. The narrator can be the volcano waiting to erupt or the polar bear stranded on a glacier. Think of being a small entity in these monumental places and write big and bold, so your audience will feel as if they were there too.

Donna J. Sanders

A Season of Delicious Thoughts

Relax this week and enjoy the food, family and friends for the holidays. Have fun making snow angels if you live in a winter wonderland. Show your appreciation for the thoughtful gifts. Help grandma with the kitchen duties if she has been working hard to prepare all day. But if you get bored or need to escape the chaos, you can always take a moment to write, as the season is filled with so many delicious thoughts.

You walk into a house full of noise; every member of the family talking over each other. You already miss the silence. Take it as a cue to go admire the decorations inside or get some fresh air amidst nature. Compare the sounds you are trying to escape with pleasant ones from outside or the soft music in the background. Match up a few family members to the ornaments on a Christmas tree. Oh what fun it will be to write a few whimsical poems of what your twisted mind sees.

The food was a delight and you stuffed yourself with turkey, ham, green beans and a few extra bites. You had to unbuckle your belt to breathe. You escape to a room where you can lay down for a short while. But you are still thinking about the dessert table you might attack in a few; except for that heavy fruit cake! The way it looks is how you feel right about now. Write a poem from the fruitcake's perspective. Perhaps it feels lonely and unwanted like so many single people you know. And those cookies; why are they always the first to go? They are the popular kids. Write if you were one of them or the outcast.

When the gift giving is in session, take advantage of your observation skills. Look at the faces people make as they open each present. Pay attention to the way each one is wrapped and who it was from. How does the choice of color and pattern compare to their personality? How do the children react and play with the toys they get? What are the pets in the house doing as the festivities are occurring? There can be so much literature that can read like a Dr. Seuss book in these moments.

Engage in your family traditions. It may seem uninteresting to you, having done it year after year, but to write about some of the unusual ways you celebrate can be intriguing to someone else. What distinct foods are cooked for the holidays? Describe the process of the day and maybe play around with what the outcome would be if it was out of order. What kind of theme is used on the Christmas tree at each house you have been to every year? Indulge in how each tradition came about.

Do you spend time catching up with the people you don't see often during the holidays? Who are the outcasts in the family…maybe engage in a conversation and learn something you didn't know about their lives. Go clown around at the kids table and write about the funny things they say. If a nephew has decided to invite his new girlfriend to the festivities, try to figure out her personality by the way she is dressed and observing her body language. Then get to know her a little better and compare the before and after thoughts to create a poem.

Not everyone is able to enjoy the holidays. Put yourself in their shoes and write about what they might be going through. There are still millions of homeless who may not have a hot meal. There are those who distance themselves from society during this time of year, so they don't feel even more depressed. There are soldiers still fighting, and those who have to refrain from noise and bright lights because of PTSD. While we stuff our faces and cozy up next to a fire, feel for those who have been burdened with unfortunate circumstances.

The season is filled with so much to write about. It may get a little hectic with all the shopping, cooking and decorating, but take some time in between to write about the experiences. They are memories after all; so why not immortalize them with words?

Donna J. Sanders

Different Types of Writing Can Benefit You

We all know that budding writers are in pursuit of being published. Indeed, many of us share that common goal, whether for the first time or the tenth time. But sometimes too little attention is given to the power of writing as a kind of personal, solitary fulfillment and the benefits it can provide us both professionally and mentally. This should be just as important for each of us as our final goal.

We are not merely talking about stories or poems here: writing can bring you personal benefits in many forms that go beyond your creative side yet help to assist it, such as by providing new ideas or lessons on grammar. Diaries, journals, plot outlines, lists, essays, letter ... just about anything that requires a pen and paper and the written word will fit the description. You might be writing to improve your memory, to learn, to give yourself reminders, and so on.

It is the activity of writing (and not necessarily the act of writing creatively) that we are discussing here. Why? Well, writing is a skill that develops over time and with plenty of practice, which, as they say, makes perfect. Honing your punctuation, grammar and proofreading skills, for instance, can be done really well in non or less creative forms of writing. Keeping a journal or diary is a good way to improve your memory, which will come in handy when you have something long to write or think up a great line with five hours left to go at work or school – and nowhere handy to write it down. And writing every day is, of course, good practice.

Writing can also benefit your mental health. On the basest level, it allows you to take the thoughts within your mind and express them in the written form, whether with or without the use of metaphorical devices. This can be particularly helpful for those of us who regularly feel stressed out or find our thoughts getting in the way of our daily lives and our writing goals. If you can get these thoughts out of your mind, then (who knows!) you may be removing the one thing that is preventing you from writing a masterpiece. Personal writing can be a way for us to get these issues off our chests and provide us with a sense of satisfaction.

It is not easy to write every single day, especially not for those of us who are focused on our creativity or producing something that will catch the attention of an agent or a publisher. But alternative methods of everyday writing can provide an outlet during moments of – let's call it "Writer's Block" – and provide our writing skills a boost along the way.

Laura Marie Clark

Missed Opportunities

Time stops when one is unemployed. I no longer have to set an alarm to get to work on time, I can do my chores anytime of the week and I don't get impatient in the lines at the store. When life slows down a few notches, you also tend to be more observant at the objects surrounding you. It hasn't been very fun without a paycheck every week, but it has given me a new outlook at all the things I have been missing out as a writer.

At the unemployment center a few weeks ago, I was mesmerized by the most beautiful Tabebuia tree at their front entrance. I dreaded going to the place for an orientation session, but the tree left quite an impression on me that I ended up bringing my good digital camera on my next trip so I could capture its beauty at all angles. The tree's trunk and branches twisted like a serpent and with spring finally in Florida, it flourished with hundreds of its bright yellow, trumpet-shaped flowers. I research the tree's history, as I never knew its name even though I saw them every day at my apartment complex, and was inspired to write a poem about it. I not only gained knowledge, but I was able to use my gift to create something beautiful.

I think back about how many missed opportunities there were during my daily travels. How many other moments in nature I didn't see because I was too angry with the drivers in front of me or that homeless man on the median who probably has quite a story to tell? What about the tender moments between siblings at a park or those dry leaves left over from winter flowing into the sewers? Everything we see has the potential to become poetry or a chapter in a book. Never again will I take the little things for granted and even if I don't get the chance to write about them, at least I was able to see them with appreciative eyes.

Donna J. Sanders

Stories in the Media

As writers, we get our inspiration from many places, including (although we may not always want to admit it) from other people's stories. Why should the newspaper or the internet be any different?

You can find a variety of stories in the media that you can take ideas from or expand upon when you write. The articles that you find can inspire you to create a more complete tale, change the ending to send a moral message, or select a specific fact from the article to discuss.

Taking a popular subject area can allow you to highlight your opinion on an important issue and spark a discussion. You can use sensitive issues in your poetry or stories, or even construct a persuasive argument in a more formal way. Being able to produce a strong argument is an excellent writing skill for you to master. What you create can be about your feelings when you first read the story, the impact you believe it must have had on those involved, or a retelling. There is so much information out there to read that you will probably find no end of stories that inspire you.

Be careful when you take a story from the media to use in your own writing: ensure that you do not copy it and instead try to fictionalize it. Change names and places and any other information that could be considered necessary, and if necessary reference where you got your inspiration from.

Laura Marie Clark

Senses

It's easy to use sight in our writing. We can describe what our characters are doing, how they are behaving and what they look like. We can describe the beauty of one scene or the grim emptiness of another. It is far harder to get our readers to smell, taste, touch and hear, but these are things that we should focus on when were are writing in order to fully immerse the audience into what we have created.

Using the example of a waterfall, let's take a look at using the five senses.

1. Sight

The easiest sense to write about. Describe how the water cascades down the side of a cliff, frothing at the bottom. It hits the rocks there and small droplets of water fly off onto the grass on the bank. The water is clear. Though it moves quickly down the cliff, the pool below is still.

2. Sound

This sense, too, can be simple to use. Consider what you would be able to hear if you stood close to the waterfall. Try to be specific rather than using simple words like quiet and loud. Does the water thunder against the rocks? In contrast, what can you hear near the pool? In the wider scene, are the animals calling to one another, or is the silence strange compared to the deafening sound of the waterfall?

3. Touch

Now let's imagine you can reach out and touch this waterfall. You run your fingers through the running water. Describe whether it is cool or warm, weak or powerful, and so on. The rocks are slippery and rough; the droplets that fly off them splatter on your face.

4. Taste

Now you're going to drink the water. It may look refreshing, but is that how it actually tastes? What do you feel as it slides down your throat? Again, be detailed: explain whether something is sweet enough to leave your mouth watering or so bitter that the nasty taste remains on your tongue for hours afterwards?

5. Smell

The waterfall is a natural phenomenon. What can you smell there? Animals are around you – perhaps one of them has been in the pool and you can smell the wet scent of them. Can you smell the froth at the bottom of the waterfall?

We use these senses all the time in our daily lives, and our readers do the same. You can place your reader directly within your writing by providing them with each of these senses.

Laura Marie Clark

Listen to Your Words

Often as a writer we type our story or poetry and are anxious to share it with other people to receive feedback. Before sharing your work in a public forum you should read it out loud, yes out loud, a minimum of ten times. Our reading mind often matches our writing mind, and we read our work as we intended to write it flaws and all because we know what we were trying to convey, but others might not.

When we vocalize our work and read it as we intend it to be read and interpreted several times out loud we are able to recognize areas of our work that may not flow properly, words that are misused, line breaks in our stanzas, etc.

Listen to the way your words flow. Make sure you are conveying the story your writing mind intended. Read your work out loud a minimum of ten times. If the flow is good and no editing needs to be made, by all means share it. If you need to edit your work, make the changes and start the process over. Listen to your words, speak them out loud.

Raja Williams

Set Realistic Targets

We all want to write as much as we possibly can and as professionally as we can, but unfortunately other things in our lives can get in the way. Work, school, homework, cleaning, cooking … there's an endless list of things that you may feel prevent you from sitting down and writing as often as you might like. It can be frustrating when you can't find enough time to pursue your creative desires.

A great way to feel accomplished despite the limited time you have is to set yourself good targets. For instance, if you're working Monday to Friday from 9 to 5, it is unlikely that you'll be able to write 5,000 words of your novel every day. You won't create 20 poems a week, either. Make realistic targets for yourself, such as:

- 2 or 3 blog posts per week.
- 500 words a day.
- 30 minutes of focused writing a day.
- Writing in response to 1 or 2 prompts per week.

By setting yourself small goals, you will not push yourself to write more than you are able, and you will be able to focus on the standard of your writing more than simply producing something. When you meet (or even beat) these targets, you will enjoy a sense of accomplishment with your writing.

Laura Marie Clark

Pruning The Weeds

You've planted many seeds with your ink; watched your sentences bloom and flourish, but now it looks a bit crowded on the page. Now what?

When our closets get a bit cluttered, we finally do that spring cleaning we put off for many seasons. When our refrigerator it too full of old, expired foods, we get rid of the products leaving bad odors. When our gardens are overrun by overgrown weeds, we must prune those unwelcomed guests.

The same goes for writing. Whether you are working on a novel, short story or poem, pruning is an important part of the process. The second phase should be when you take the time to remove those repetitive verbs, unnecessary adjectives and overused clichés. It may take reading the same paragraph or page over and over again, but it must be done.

Don't be ashamed to use a dictionary to refresh your mind with the meaning of words, or a thesaurus to replace a few. You can swallow your pride and ask friends or family who are teachers and writers (if they are willing), to be a second pair of eyes for your work. Others may see what we miss in the editing process.

In his book On Writing Well, William Zinsser suggests using brackets to recognize clutter and his reason for using them:

"I would put brackets around every component in a piece of writing that wasn't doing useful work.... Sometimes my brackets surround an entire sentence – the one that essentially repeats what the previous sentence said, or that says something readers don't need to know or can figure out themselves. Most first drafts can be cut by 50 percent without losing any information or losing the author's voice.

My reason for bracketing the students' superfluous words, instead of crossing them out, was to avoid violating their sacred prose. I wanted to leave the sentence intact for them to analyze."

Zinsser's idea was to simplify but also appreciate all the words that had to be discarded. And never use them like corporations and politicians do, to mislead an audience – a concept he calls "verbal camouflage."

Some of the things we write just need a good cleansing. So instead of grabbing an eraser, white out or using the delete button, put those useless snippets in brackets or off to the side. You never know if you could use them later in another phase of the writing process.

Donna J. Sanders

Source: Zinsser, William. On Writing Well. New York: Collins, 2006. 14-16. Print

Obsessions Have Power

She was a writer who had an intense love for birds, peacocks in particular. As a child, she taught a chicken to walk backwards and became a media sensation. She had pheasants, quail, turkeys, geese and ducks. Some of them she weaved into her writing and her obsession would leave an odd legacy among many other writers with strange habits. Flannery O'Connor was an American writer who wrote in a Southern Gothic style, combining the grotesque with Christian Realism.

I intend to stand firm and let the peacocks multiply, for I am sure that, in the end, the last word will be theirs. –Flannery O'Connor

In today's society, we have become obsessed with trends whether it is the most popular TV show or the latest diet craze. Some obsessions can be collecting trinkets, helping animals in need or shopping for clothes. As writers, we can channel those obsessions and use them in our writing as O'Connor did.

An obsession of a theme can be our muse for writing poetry, short stories or novels. William Wordsworth often wrote about nature; Philip K. Dick delved into Science Fiction for his many short stories; and Stephen King sticks to the macabre for most of his novels. Whatever genre you write in, integrate your obsessions into your work.

Natalie Goldberg suggests making a list of our obsessions and put them to good use. When you are inspired, go back to the list and harness the power of each one to write:

And your main obsessions have power; they are what will come back to in your writing over and over again. And you'll create new stories around them.

So you might as well give in to them. They probably take over your life whether you want them to or not, so you ought to get them to work for you. - Goldberg, Writing Down the Bones

If you love sports, use it as a metaphor for a trial you have faced or a struggle you are dealing with today. If you are obsessed with the beach, inhale the atmosphere and write a descriptive poem. From that collection of rare books, you can pluck elements of their worth into a fictional story. Let those obsessions seep into your soul and violate your veins until the energy inside needs to be released. Obsessions have power, so don't let them go to waste.

Donna J. Sanders

Sources: Goldberg, Natalie. Writing Down the Bones. Boston: Shambhala, 2005. Print (42)

Popova, Maria. "The Odd Habits and Curious Customs of Famous Writers." brainpickings. Web, 2 November 2015. https://www.brainpickings.org/2013/09/23/odd-type-writers/

Schiffer, Kathy. "Flannery's Peacocks: "King of the Birds" Run Amok." patheos. 5 June 2015. Web, 2 November 2015.
http://www.patheos.com/blogs/kathyschiffer/2015/06/flannerys-peacocks-king-of-the-birds-run-amok/

http://www.georgiaencyclopedia.org/articles/arts-culture/flannery-oconnor-1925-1964

From Trash To Treasure

When we move or spring clean, how many times have we sorted through our belongings to find things we consider insignificant or trash but then someone else finds value in it after buying it at a garage sale or picking it up from your garbage pile? An old rickety chair can be restored with a little tender loving care. A discolored vase can turn out to be an antique worth a lot. It can be the same with writing.

I can't tell you how many notebooks I have with unfinished stories and poems I don't think are worth sharing. I never discard anything I write because I feel that something good could come from it later on. I could be inspired to revise my stories or take a snippet from a poem and make something fresh and new.

Those five to ten minute free writing exercises can be gibberish to some, but I find them exhilarating; a way to get a lot of emotions onto paper that we don't often find the time to release. By reviewing them a few days or even a few weeks later, one can possibly find inspiration to construct a poem or expand on the idea written.

Natalie Goldberg calls this concept "composting." In her book Writing Down the Bones, she explains:

Our bodies are garbage heaps: we collect experience, and from the decomposition of the thrown-out eggshells, spinach leaves, coffee grinds, and old steak bones of our minds come nitrogen, heat, and very fertile soil. Out of this fertile soil bloom our poems and stories. But this does not come all at once. It takes time. Continue to turn over and over the organic details of your life until some of them fall through the garbage of discursive thoughts to the solid ground of black soil. (15)

Writing Tips - Volume 1

What we write is like tending a garden. We bury the seeds in soil, water and fertilize them hoping that something sprouts. We want our harvest to be edible for hungry minds but we also throw out the rotten fruit left to decay on the ground. The writing we may think is garbage could be the words someone else needs to hear.

So go ahead and share that poem you think might not be appealing. Share that story you may consider nonsense. But never throw out anything you write, because your trash could be another's treasure.

Donna J. Sanders

Source: Goldberg, Natalie. Writing Down the Bones. Boston: Shambhala, 2005. Print

Revitalize The World

Lately, it seems as if the world is turning inside out: attacks on human life almost every day, many natural disasters changing the landscape of our planet, countries at war, and people just losing hope. Technology has made it easy to find out within seconds, any event from anywhere in the world. The media feeds off the carnage and it is hard to escape. Some of us even refuse to turn on the television to avoid the horrific news.

As one of those people who use to loathe history, politics and any kind of chaos, I have realized how important it is not only to stay informed, but to use all of it as inspiration for my writing.

Most poets write from the discord within, as a sort of therapy to heal themselves. Why can't we do the same with the pandemonium we see from outside sources? Some poets give historical descriptions of wars experienced, preferring to express angst. Pablo Neruda did so with the Spanish civil war, as well as Paul Celan, a survivor of the Holocaust. Teresa Mei ChucTeresa Mei Chuc, a Vietnamese poet who migrated to the U.S. after the Vietnam War, gives readers a different perspective. She writes compassionately of her experiences while giving us a glimpse into the history and culture of her country.

As much as we poets love to express our opinions on politics and war, as it often stirs up controversy and will get readers into heated discussions, write from the heart as Chuc does to show another perspective of strife. She uses her poetry to heal the time lost from her country of birth. With her poem "Praying at the Cemetery on Con Son Island," she attempts to reconnect with the people and traditions of the land while visiting a gravesite:

Some graves were marked with a yellow star and a name, many others were marked by a yellow star but no name because the person dead could not be identified. Everywhere I looked in all directions, as far as my eyes could see, were gravestones of people who died on the island from the wars, including those who died during imprisonment during the most recent U.S. war in Vietnam. I offered incense and prayers for peace and love for these souls.

Lives are lost every day whether from war, domestic crime, natural disasters, or poor health. Instead of focusing on the melancholy of death, write an uplifting poem of the victim or a beautiful moment that occurred after. Use the memories of a person seen in a news article or emphasize the act of the heroes involved. When nature intervenes, describe a place of the way it used to be or its significance in history and culture. Write to give others hope rather than dampen spirits. It is what people need today more than ever, and as poets, we can have a bigger impact by revitalizing the soul.

Donna J. Sanders

Sources: Chuc, Teresa Mei. "Vietnamese Globe: Divided by War, United by Poetry and Compassion." Dissident Voice. 6 July, 2015. Web, 7 December 2015.
http://dissidentvoice.org/2015/07/vietnamese-globe-divided-by-war-united-by-poetry-and-compassion/

A Classic Story Finds Life Again

We artists – we create. We can take the hideous parts of life and turn it into something beautiful; something seen from a different perspective through another's eyes. We are also curious. We wonder why things work; constantly questioning the elements that guide and motivate us.

One author explored the aspects of life, beauty, and curiosity in a gothic tale that still influences the world today.

This Thanksgiving, a new generation will get to know Victor Frankenstein and his creation from another perspective. The story is told from his assistant Igor's point-of-view, and delves into the scientist's transition into madness, as he toils over the monstrous being roaming the world freely.

If you read the classic novel by Mary Shelley, you would know that Victor did not have such an assistant and the character was created for Hollywood's early versions of the story. It has also been misconstrued that the creature's name was Frankenstein, when it was in fact the name of his creator. Throughout the novel he was known as the "demon," "monster," and even referred to as "it."

Victor Frankenstein was a student of chemistry and alchemy, and soon becomes obsessed with creating life. He manages to assemble a humanoid by unearthing corpses and uses the elements of science to bring it to life. However, he is filled with fear and regret after seeing how hideous the creature is. The creature shows empathy by longing for a companion, but Victor is afraid of what will come if he brings another monster to life. The monster seeks revenge by murdering those close to him and Victor hunts the creature till his death.

The story contains a lot of components relative to humanity even today. While Victor saw his creation to be hideous, the creature was able to find compassion from a blind man. It teaches us that beauty is not always seen, but can be felt. And we humans are always quick to judge a book by its cover rather than discover what is within.

The monster longed for someone to love and to love him, but by being denied that love, he chose the path of murderous revenge. The lack of acceptance by society led him into darkness. They saw him as an evil thing, and it is what he became. There are too many times we pass by those who just want to be acknowledged or to fit in. A little kindness can have big impact on a soul filled with turmoil.

Being curious may not always be a good thing. The story teaches us that some aspects of science should not be tampered with. Victor did not consider the consequences of his experiment and expressed his regret over and over again. He released a being mankind was not ready for, but was smart enough not to share his secret, for fear another may replicate his work.

What you can be curious of is the real story of Victor Frankenstein and his monster. It doesn't matter how many film versions you have seen, Shelley's marvelous science fiction tale examines the relationship between man and monster with such depth; one cannot help but feel sorry for both. So scour those shelves or go grab a copy from the library, and indulge in one of the greatest novels ever written.

Donna J. Sanders

Sources: Shelley, Mary. Frankenstein. London: Penguin Books, 1992. pg. 58. Print.

An Epic Lesson

The word "epic" has been way overused in our time; often hearing or reading it when someone uses the word to describe a movie or an event. I have been guilty myself using it a few times but I am proud to say I know of its origins, having studied Beowulf, The Epic of Gilgamesh and The Iliad in many of my literature courses.

The Oxford Dictionary defines "epic" as:

"A long poem, typically one derived from ancient oral tradition, narrating the deeds and adventures of heroic or legendary figures or the history of a nation."

and it's origins: Late 16th century (as an adjective): via Latin from Greek epikos, from epos 'word, song', related toeipein 'say'.

To sum it up – one of the longest poems you will ever read, about the size of a novel.

In the days when men were proud to be in battle and tell tales of their journeys and adventures, narrating the account in an epic poem was the way to pass the stories down from generation to generation. These poems are often full of the history of ancient cities, legends of mythical beasts and creatures from land and sea, and the heroes who rise and eventually fall.

Though epic poems are sparse in our century, here are a few to explore from throughout the ages:

Beowulf – author unknown (8th – 10th Century)

Known as the oldest surviving poem in Old English, the story is set in Scandinavia where Beowulf, the hero of Geats, comes to the aid of the king of Danes to defeat the Grendel monster. The tale spans fifty years of the hero's life until his death. Often a difficult poem to read, the Seamus Heaney edition (pictured above) has been the easiest version to understand.

The Faerie Queene – Edmund Spenser (1596)

An allegorical poem that follows the adventures of several knights while exploring the virtues of holiness, chastity, temperance, friendship, justice, courtesy and magnificence. Spenser also includes the conflicts of religion and politics in the story, taking aim at the corruption within the Catholic Church.

Omeros – Derek Walcott (1990)

This 20th century Caribbean writer received a lot of praise for his epic poem, channeling Homer's, The Iliad, in a tale set on the island of St. Lucia. Walcott blends African culture with Greek lore, to explore the threads of humanity and its connection with history and nature. He weaves in relationships laden with wounds, ending the story by delving into his own poetic consciousness. The epic poem can be an interesting read if you give it a try. Not entirely historical fact, but these nostalgic tales can provide some insight into cultures, tribes and even legendary figures. You could compare it to reading a fairy tale or science fiction story, but in poetic form. It can be quite a task to write one and definitely would be a challenge for any writer.

Donna J. Sanders

Sources: •https://www.poets.org/poetsorg/text/poets-glossary-epic
•http://www.oxforddictionaries.com/us/definition/american_english/epic

Graveyard Poetry

Now that Halloween is over, we'll probably not see any more poems about the dark and morbid right? Absolutely incorrect!

Our pain and scars can be riddled with darkness. Some of our most traumatic events are morbid in our eyes. The poems we often write – the ones that rise from the deepest places in our soul to capture and question the elements of human nature – are what some would classify as graveyard poetry.

The graveyard genre stemmed from the eighteenth century in the form of British poetry, delving into the macabre to question the mortality of man. The poets who dabbled deeply into graveyards and death where highly criticized for such themes, but their work would have great influence later in the Gothic Literature and Romanticism periods.

Thomas Parnell, who is noted as writing the first graveyard poem "A Night-Piece on Death," explores how death should not be feared as it is a necessity. Parnell uses the symbolism of chains to represent the burdens and limits of man the mortal, and once those chains are removed, all men are equal. The different sizes of the headstones observed indicate the social status of those who are buried, but death puts us all on the same level. Fame is no longer important in the afterlife.

While graveyard poets wrote about a lonely wanderer or the death of ordinary men, poets today often connect the humans we come across with a bag of bones or walking zombies. Death can be the loss of our old selves, we can mourn for our souls in the midst of heartbreak, and we can even write about the turmoil haunting our dreams. The graveyard can be a metaphor for our emotions, human alienation or even the changes in our world.

Even though we have removed the masks after a night of tricks and treats, we humans still have many layers beneath filled with emotions that stir and disturb our slumber. As poets, to find some solidarity, those thoughts have to be put to death. So we carve them onto tombstones to remind those wandering in graveyards that poetry is how we break free from those chains, if only for a brief moment.

Donna J. Sanders

Sources: http://www.self.gutenberg.org/articles/graveyard_poets

A Love For Literature

It has not been easy in the job market for many, including myself. I have been doing office work for years because it is where my experience lies, but I always knew it wasn't what I was meant to do. I went to college with the intentions of being a teacher, but it is more difficult to get into the field without any classroom hours or experience.

When people ask me what my degree was in, I can sense the disapproval and lack of confidence that my choice will not benefit my chances. I chose to study literature because of my love for reading and writing. I don't regret it for one minute because I was able to learn so much and delve into such a variety of artists I never knew existed.

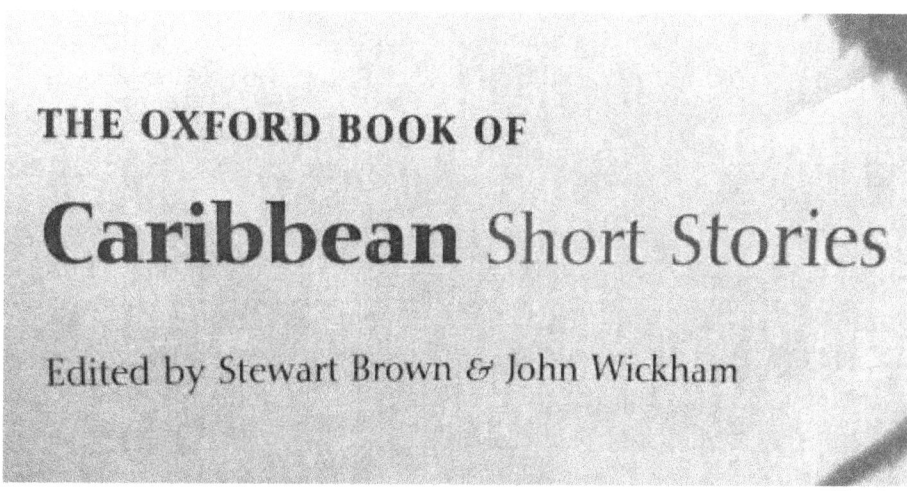

I was surprised to see a Caribbean Literature class available, and being from the islands, it never occurred to me that many award winning artists came from all over the Caribbean. I studied Derek Walcott, Earl Lovelace, V.S Naipaul, Edwidge Danticat and Maryse Conde, to name a few. I kept every single book used for the class. One of my favorites is The Oxford Book of Short Stories, an anthology of stories from authors all over the Caribbean and a few from South America.

I was fortunate to study Gothic literature, one of my favorite genres. The curriculum included: Frankenstein, Dracula, several poems and stories from Edgar Allan Poe, and even the story regarded as the first gothic novel – The Castle of Otranto. But it was a poem from Samuel Taylor Coleridge that would intrigue me the most. "The Rime of the Ancient Mariner" from the romantic era, is a lengthy tale of a sailor's many experiences during his long sea voyage. It is the author's longest written poem published in his collection Lyrical Ballads.

With an intense love for everything Science Fiction, I was able to take a class dedicated to work of Philip K. Dick. Already a fan of the movie versions of his stories: Total Recall, Minority Report, Imposter, Screamers and Blade Runner, it was exciting to hold in depth discussions regarding the psychological and political aspects of his twisted tales. Dick combines mental illness and autism, with the physics of time in Martian Time-Slip. It is an intriguing tale about humans colonizing Mars, where capitalism and a disregard for humanity remains the same as it does on Earth. Dick was definitely an author ahead of his time with the way he foresaw the future of humanity's demise.

His work was so fascinating; I ended up writing my Master's thesis using a few of his stories. Titled "Mechanized Humans: Our Future Predicted by Philip K. Dick," I dug deep into Martian Time-Slip, UBIK, Do Androids Dream of Electric Sleep and Second Variety, to reveal that Dick was giving a warning to mankind as he saw technology taking humanity down a road where all empathy would soon be revoked.

If you love to read like I do, you might be amazed to find authors from your roots. My husband is part Irish, and I was able to share some Irish poets with him during my school endeavors. I love many aspects of the Asian culture, and often I will come across wonderful poems and stories from different countries of the East while doing research on recipes and food.

There is an entire world of literature out there at the tip of our fingers. I will never be ashamed of choosing to study such an important art and don't let anyone tell you it is a useless degree. My love for the written word will pay off one day and I don't plan on giving up on that dream anytime soon.

Donna J. Sanders

Let Your Poetry Be Open To Interpretation

Let Your Poetry Be Open To Interpretation

Poetry is all about the reader's experience. You may have an idea in mind that you wish to convey, and they may have a similar experience to you that the poem reminds them of, or they may feel particularly affected by your poetry in the way that you desired. Your reader may also react in a way you did not imagine – with a memory of something important to them or an alternate emotion, based on an image or a word that you have used. One of the most wonderful things about poetry is that it can be open to interpretation.

This is something you should use when you are writing. Allowing people to interpret your poetry does not mean that you need to be less specific when you are writing. If there is a subject you really feel you need to write about (and there are many out there), then go ahead and write about it as passionately as you are able. You can be as specific or as obscure as you wish, providing your creation allows people to interpret it in their own way.

Use poetic devices in order to leave your poetry open to interpretation. Simile and metaphor are excellent ways to conjure imagery that can affect people. The senses will allow them to experience it and can help to create emotions. Building upon these emotions can provide your reader with their own understanding as well as yours, granting them their own opportunities to interpret the words. By allowing your poetry to be open to interpretation, you include your readers and their own experiences in that work.

Laura Marie Clark

Poetry: Know Your Purpose

There will always be a reason behind what you are writing. Sometimes, poetry is as simple as celebrating the ordinary and every day. It does not always have to be concerned with epic adventures or glorious renditions of love. The purpose of a poem can be grand or small.

When you write poetry, your purpose is projected onto the page. Do you want to recognize the beauty in something that most people think nothing of? The beauty of your favorite food or drink; the beauty of coming home after work or school every day to a loving family; the beauty of merely celebrating who you are. All of these things are worthy topics to focus on: you don't have to write a deep piece of poetry in order to present a meaningful purpose.

On the other hand, your purpose could be much larger and bolder. You might want to highlight something you believe is wrong with society or something that people are not comfortable with talking about so that your readers might take notice of these issues. Or, you might want to celebrate a great national or international event, commemorate a special day, or remember a moment in history. Again, you can encourage your readers to think about these things when they read your poem. Writing poetry with a purpose does not mean that you need a powerful message hidden between the lines. It can be obvious in its simplicity, and your subjects can be widespread. Your purpose, whether personal or otherwise, can really help your poem to stand out.

Laura Marie Clark

To Rhyme or Not To Rhyme?

An important thing to consider when you are writing poetry is whether the poem should or should not rhyme. It is something you should decide on at the beginning, before you create your poem or before it takes on a noticeable form. There are advantages and disadvantages to both of these. Let's take a look.

To Rhyme!

Rhyming provides an easy way for you to create a clear sense of rhythm in your piece. You will probably find yourself using a more solid form if you rhyme, with lines of similar length to maintain a pattern. However, it can also restrict you when you write. When you choose to rhyme, you limit yourself to a specific number of words at the end of each line. To make it easier, you can use near rhymes as well as perfect rhymes. "Strong" and "wrong" are examples of perfect rhymes; "strong" and "string" are examples of near rhymes, because they sound similar (the -ng sound) without being full rhymes. You would also have the choice to use a specific form of poetry such as limerick if you wish.

Not to Rhyme!

Choosing not to rhyme in your poem provides you with the possibility to write more freely on your chosen subject and there is less chance that it will become skewered by a distinct lack of rhyming words available to you. However, the biggest challenge comes when you try to create a distinct rhythm in the piece. You have to consider carefully where one line should end and the next one begin. When done correctly, you can create a wonderful, flowing piece of poetry that can have a considerable impact on your audience.

Laura Marie Clark

Poetry: How Long is a Line?

You pick up your pen
And begin
To write with ingenious intention
To create a poem
Of wit
Or of rhyme
Or of passion –
But hold on
Something is terribly wrong!
Where should you put
Your line breaks?

And where should you
Start
Or end
A new verse?
Ah, fret not!

Unless limited
To a form such as haiku
There's no need to fear

As you write, think
What do I wish to
Emphasise
In this poetic enterprise?
How should my poem sound
When
A stranger reads it out loud?
And when a line becomes too long
Think
How can I divide this line up into smaller,
individual lines
in order to keep the flow of my poem both natural and enticing?

The answer is entirely
Up to you

So read, explore,
Create!
And I hope you found this silly tip
More useful
Than a paragraph telling you
To think carefully about
The structure
Of your poetry.

Laura Marie Clark

Rhythm in Poetry

I have discussed rhythm in poetry many times. The best free form poetry has a solid, strong rhythm that does not falter throughout. It can flow from one pattern to another, drifting from a fast pace to a slow pace, but the transition has been cleverly thought through and tested by the author. Poems with a stricter form have a sense of rhythm already, but this can fall apart if the language does not reflect the form or words have been squashed into sentences to make them fit.

So how exactly can you examine the rhythm of your poem?

The challenge for any poet or budding poet is to write something that sounds natural and flows. This includes using powerful lines to impact your readers and choosing where to place your line breaks carefully. If you put a line break in the wrong place, your poem may sound false and fall apart.
 It is not always easy to create a good rhythm. The rules are up to you and depend on what you have written. No two people will agree and what one person thinks has rhythm may mean nothing to someone else. But you, as the writer, should know the rhythm of your poem and feel it flowing through your work.

When you have written a new poem, try taking it apart and removing line breaks or changing key words in your piece. Throw in some alliteration or repetition of key phrases. This may result in large changes to the poem. Does it alter the mood of your poem, too? Does it feel easier or harder to read? You do not want your readers to become confused at the end of a line if it does not flow properly onto the next. Take it apart again and move things around some more. Ask yourself how the rhythm has changed and which form of the poem you prefer. You may discover a new rhythm that you will want to use again and again.

Laura Marie Clark

Playful Poetry

Remember when your parents would tell you not to play with your food? It's very hard for a budding young writer not to, with dishes like alphabet soup. Many chefs even get playful by making their culinary creations into art for presentation. So why couldn't we bend the rules a little with writing, to create playful poetry?

Many profound artists have used humor in their writing. Shakespeare's comedic tale "Much Ado About Nothing" involved trickery and eavesdropping amidst a twisted kind of romance. Within the psychology and horror of Edgar Allan Poe's work lies a bit of humorous irony hidden in stories such as, "The Black Cat." In the tale, a cat the protagonist loathes and was attempting to murder, reveals a hideous crime he was trying to conceal.

Award winning author, Erica Jong (Fear of Flying) often chooses to write about female sexuality, but in her poetry collection Love Comes First, she decides to focus on love and other little tidbits of her life. Nestled in between is a witty poem called "The Poem Cat," where she symbolically compares the wandering pet to finding inspiration.

When many of think of playful poetry, Shel Silverstein probably comes to mind. In books like Where the Sidewalk Ends, for a more youthful audience, he often includes clever illustrations. Not only is it visually stimulating, the poems contain humor and are very sincere. Many adults are still drawn to his work, often passing on their love for his poetry to the next generation.

Modern artists like Tristan Fitzgerald, have been using social media sites like Instagram to share illustrated work. Fitzgerald combines his artwork with the written word to create an interesting array of posts on his page. With over 5000 followers and still growing, his creations are unique and entertaining.

If your writing needs some refreshing, maybe it's time to think outside of the box and tweak the formulas you are used to. Throw out the rules of spelling and grammar, and be a little playful with your words. Unusual methods have worked for a few artists, and maybe it can lead to creating a whole new style no one has seen before.

Donna J. Sanders

Repetition in Poetry

There are many ways to use repetition in poetry. Each type of repetition can have a different impact on the way that your writing sounds and have a different effect on your readers. It can help writers to list for effect and emphasize particular words, emotions or phrases within your poetry. Let's look at some different ways to use repetition.

Anaphora

This is the repetition of a word or a phrase at the beginning of a clause.
"We shall fight on the beaches, we shall fight on the landing grounds, we shall fight in the fields and in the streets, we shall fight in the hills, we shall never surrender." – Winston Churchill

Epistrophe

Similar to anaphora, this is the repetition of a word or a phrase at the end of a clause.

"Where now? Who now? When now?" – The Unnamable, Samuel Beckett

Epizeuxis

This is the repetition of the same word or phrase in succession.

"Alone, alone, all, all alone,
 Alone on a wide, wide sea"
 – The Rime of the Ancient Mariner

Anadiplosis

This is the repetition of the last word of a clause as the first word of the next clause.

"This, it seemed to him, was the end, the end of a world as he had known it…"
– James Oliver Curwood

Laura Marie Clark

Concrete Words and Images

We have previously discussed that poetry is about feelings and the senses. Therefore, your readers need to be presented with images and things that are concrete: words that are specific. A concrete word is a noun. It describes something that you can experience with the senses, such as something you can see (smoke), something you can hear (a cry) or something you can touch (skin). They help us to explain something to someone else.

Concrete words are useful in poetry (and other forms of writing) because they provide readers with an example of something that they can understand. Although we might associate different memories with them, they are things that everyone has experienced (or will experience). This means that when you create a metaphor, you can present a stronger image to the reader than if you use abstract words to describe something.

Abstract words and words that name qualities. They do not have a physical form, but describe ideas or concepts and are not available to our senses. Examples are beauty, lies and democracy. These are not things that we can reach out and touch. They are things that mean different things to different people and can change meaning over time (whereas concrete words, such as 'table', do not tend to change meaning).

Your poetry may be about abstract topics. You may wish to discuss some moral lesson or philosophy. You may want to write about a feeling you have or your favorite memory. Describing these things using concrete imagery can make them clearer for your readers. It will allow you to create more powerful descriptions of things that we cannot see, touch, taste, hear or smell, and introduce your readers to how you view the concept you have chosen to write about.

Laura Marie Clark

Visual Poetry

In the techno savvy world we live in today, you would think it would be easier to share your writing and gain a plethora of followers on social media sites. Not always the case in my experience, so one has to come up with more creative ways to attract that target audience.

I find that just posting the text of a poem brings minimal results, and it doesn't help that certain sites only allow a certain amount of characters for each post. Many people today have to be visually stimulated to become interested in the writing on the wall – so to speak. I started using photos from the Internet that fit with the themes of my poems, but then I was informed of copyright infringements – so you have to be careful which photos to choose and make sure they are royalty free and give proper credit to the photographer or get permission from a photographer you might know.

I took it a step further and decided to utilize my free time and love for photography to create a make-shift studio and produce my own photographs. My creative juices started flowing when I researched how easy it was to make a light-box and I started off with a cardboard box, white tissue paper, a couple painters' lamps and white poster board. Since then I have upgraded my 20×12 box into a 30×20 pvc frame covered in white fabric and added a few more lamps. A Google search will give you all the different ways you can make one or you can even purchase them in different sizes depending on the space you have.

The fun part is just using any objects around the house to practice with: from office supplies to decorative trinkets, food, flowers, leaves – whatever themes would work for your poems – and not just literally, but symbolically as well. You can then play with the photos if you have any Photoshop skills and paste your poetry and sites onto the photo.

There are also numerous phone apps where you can upload the photos to various social media sites. The one I use is Photogrid, where I can upload directly to my Instagram, Facebook, Tumblr and Twitter accounts. The results have been quite rewarding with the responses I have gained, and I have been able to reach out to the community of writers and artists who are blossoming in the same way.

Most importantly, be inspired by the objects you see every day. Take out those smart phones and snap a photo of anything that you can write about. Let the world be your studio!

Donna J. Sanders

We All Write Bad Poems

> There once was a poet
> Who wrote a bad poem
> It was the end of a very short career

Yes, we all write bad poetry. For every poem that I feel is good enough to post online, there is a pile of screwed up pieces of paper with poor excuses for poetry scrawled across them. Nobody picks up their pen and writes a masterpiece straight away. You will (probably) never find yourself writing a large number of brilliant poems all in a row, because the skill of writing poetry is simply not that easy to perfect.

You should never be afraid of writing a bad poem. There's no pressure to allow anyone else to read it, and being unhappy with your poetry is a great way to learn what does and does not work for you. Put it to one side and take a break if you need to, or start again from the beginning. There may be one line or one verse in that poem that you like, or there may be nothing that you like at all.

The important thing is to be happy with your poetry and pick out only those things that are good and which work from the piece. It can be disappointing to write something that you are not happy with, but you should never allow yourself to be disheartened when you produce bad poetry. It does not make you a bad poet: use it to your advantage so that the next time you write, you will not make the same mistakes!

Laura Marie Clark

8 Essential Tips for Crafting and Sharing Your Poetry

1. Don't stop writing – Artists create art, Teachers teach, Writers write. To excel your writing, you need to flex your poetic muscles daily.

2. Read Poetry by other writers – By reading other writers you may find new ways to express yourself. Learn a new form, and learn what you like or do not like from the work of others.

3. Attend Open Mics – Listen to the way words are spoken. Poetry is oral just as much as it is visual genre of writing. The way a poet speaks their lines is just as important as the meaning of the lines. Open Mics are a great way for you to meet new authors, and perform your own work.

4. Study Poetic Forms – Although you may not enjoy writing sonnets, or haiku's trying various forms will help broaden your poetic development.

5. Experiment – Is there a form or rule you don't like as a writer? If so, try breaking the rule. Often the poets that are remembered were rule breakers!

6. Revise – Don't be afraid to revise your work. Revision is a great stage for experimenting with new thoughts and ideas.

7. Connect with other writers – Go to book signings, open mics, events, social media sites, anywhere you can connect with other writers. Often other poets can help you keep motivated to write and have insights to places accepting submissions or the best publishers to work with.

8. Share your work – Don't be afraid to share your work. Share it with family, friends, and other writers. Through sharing you will receive feedback to how your writing is being perceived, connect with new people, and you may even find new writing opportunities.

Raja Williams

Poetry Forms

Form: Free Verse Poetry

Free verse poetry does not follow a specific form. It is free from the constraints of traditional poetry structures and there are no specific rhyming patterns to remember: you can choose exactly what to do, how to lay it out and whether or not to rhyme. However, free verse poetry still takes on the form that you give it.

When you are writing free verse poetry, you are able to decide on the form that your poem takes. A pattern will begin to emerge as you write, whether in the rhythm, line lengths, sound or stresses. This could be based upon the feeling of your poem and the emotions you wish your readers to feel (such as short, one-worded lines for emphasis). You will establish the rules of your poem as you create it.

The line break is your ultimate tool to do this: you are free to choose when to end the line. As you are not told when to end the line in free verse poetry, this is the biggest challenge for the writer. You must make the decision about your own poem. Move line breaks around to understand the feeling of your poem and see how it can change – discover the impact that long lines and short lines have on your words and arrange them in the most effective way.

If you write a great free form poem that you love the sound or rhythm of, then don't forget to note down the form. You can always come back to it later and write another poem in that same form. Free verse poetry should not simply be created out of thin air, it should be studied and reinvented, with each line break and every word scrutinized to ensure that the best structure has been used.

Laura Marie Clark

Prose Poetry

I love reading prose poetry, but I find it very difficult to write. It sounds too much like a story and not enough like a poem when I read it back to myself. I am not alone.

Firstly, let's define prose poetry. It is poetry written as though it is prose – basically, poetry without line breaks. Although it is written in a paragraph and does not break up sentences, it maintains its poetic qualities. The poet can still use many poetic techniques including metaphor, ambiguity and powerful imagery.

A prose poetry is not a story. This is because a story will usually focus on the narrative more, whereas a prose poem will focus on poetic techniques, imagery and the general themes of poetry. To create prose poetry, you need to maintain a good rhythm throughout. This can be accomplished by ensuring that the reader is not bombarded with details or long words that can break up the flow. A prose poem tells a story to the reader through poetic techniques. Every imaged that is in the prose is there to serve a purpose, just as it should be in regular poetry. Keep a good pace and remember that you are still writing poetry, just without the line breaks.

There is a very simple way to create prose poetry. Just like when you are writing any other poem, you need to first find something that you feel needs to be said. But instead of breaking up your lines, just write the poem in one long paragraph. Play around with literary devices and you should see yourself creating something that sounds more like poetry than a story.

Prose poetry breaks the rules that we tend to associate with poetry. Some people might consider your prose more like a short story, or even just a big lump of text. If you want to write prose poetry, your job is to encourage the reader that they are still reading a poem, even though it does not look like one.

Laura Marie Clark

Response Poems

Have you ever read a quote or poem and disagreed with the contents? Don't just shake your head or roll your eyes about it. Grab your pen and paper and write a rebuttal. And even if you don't disagree with the poem, you could write an opposing view of it. Respond to the poem in an original way and make it something brand new. Response poetry is a method poets have been using for many years, and we probably don't realize we do it ourselves because there are several ways a poet can reciprocate.

Another way to respond to a poem is by using imitation. In an article written by T.S Eliot about playwright Philip Massinger, a most infamous quote taken from it reads:

One of the surest of tests is the way in which a poet borrows. Immature poets imitate; mature poets steal; bad poets deface what they take, and good poets make it into something better, or at least something different. The good poet welds his theft into a whole of feeling which is unique, utterly different from that from which it was torn; the bad poet throws it into something which has no cohesion.

Eliot insinuates one can borrow, but make sure the imitation is used to create something exclusive. A response could be to mimic another writer's form, or build a poem off a particular line or metaphor. It is not stealing if you are inspired by a word or phrase, but make it count; make it spectacular and make it your own.

A response poem can be a reply to another poem, an editorial or even a letter. Poets are always filled with questions, so why not respond to one with your own words. Pick up a newspaper and scour the editorials for something interesting and compose a poem from how you would reply. If a significant other or a grandparent writes you a letter, use it as inspiration for a poem about relationships.

You can also step out of the box when writing a response poem. Take some risks. If another poet is comparing pain to a wilted flower, take it to another level and use an object not often used to describe pain. If you have been reading multiple posts on social media about someone enjoying perfect weather or the beautiful trees in the Fall, then write a poem describing your dog's fear of thunderstorms or seeing beauty in things like a rusted car or broken eggshells. Take some time to observe the ordinary things that pass us by and use them as your muse.

Perhaps you have many poems you felt are not good enough to share. Revisit them and respond to them using the methods above; perhaps a better poem will surface. Sometimes you can pluck a few lines or phrases from your old poems to create something even more refreshing; you might be surprised by the responses you will get.

Donna J. Sanders

Freestyle

Ever had one of those moments where you just had so much to say – so many emotions stirring inside you that you just wanted to scream or take it out on someone? Then write it!! Sometimes the best poems are written because of the emotions we keep inside and we can learn to channel that energy. Put those words on paper using a freestyle strategy of writing – by letting words flow without worrying about spelling, grammar or punctuation.

Freestyle writing is a very liberating experience. Some find it as a form of therapy, like writing in a journal containing your deepest, darkest secrets. I've seen writing prompts that encourage freestyle using pictures and giving writers the choice to describe what they see, how it makes them feel or tell a story from the photo. You can even just let your pen loose by observing a waiting room at a doctor's office or watching the interactions while your kids play at the park. Or it could be as simple as taking a blank page and just writing random thoughts until they run out.

It may turn out to be a bunch of gibberish, but go back to it after a few days and it could transform into something beautiful. You may be able to pick out a few decent lines and turn it into prose. Maybe get inspired to attempt blackout poetry using markers or paint. Perhaps a soliloquy or lines of a movie script can blossom from free-styling.

Think of freestyle as a writing exercise and once you get the hang of it, then you can choose any topic to write about with ease.

Donna J. Sanders

Elegy

An elegy is a type of poem that is dedicated to the memory of someone or something special. They can be written about a loved one or an event that is surrounded by a feeling of tragedy or loss. This means that an elegy can be a very emotional piece to read or write.

The typical elegy is composed of three stages that reflect the three stages of grief:

- The first stage is lament (or sorrow), where the poet captures the emotion of their initial moment of loss. You may wish to describe what is missing from the world now that your subject has departed. You may have regrets. Or you could describe the results of a tragedy.

- The second stage is praise, where the poet admires or idolizes the subject. You may wish to celebrate how your subject will be remembered or what they did that made them unique. Use the senses to create vivid imagery in this part of the elegy.

- The third stage is acceptance, where the poet offers words of consolation or achieves peace. You may wish to focus on the lasting impact of your subject or how it will always stay with you.

Modern elegies are not always written out of a personal sense of grief. They can be in free verse or follow a more classic form, like the elegies that originated in ancient Greece.

This can be a deeply emotional form of poetry, but it does not have to be sad. Your elegy can end on a happy note as you remember the life, rather than the death (or devastation), of your subject.

Laura Marie Clark

Ode

The ode is a form of poetry that originated in Ancient Greece. It is traditionally a long poem separated into stanzas, but you can change the form as you wish. Most odes also rhyme – although how is up to you. You can also write an irregular ode without rhymes or a perfect rhythm.

An ode is a tribute to something that the poet feels particularly passionate about. This can be a person, a place, an object or an idea. The poem is defined by its theme. Odes are typically written from the poet's perspective. This is their passion. When you create an ode, you can use simile and metaphor in order to compare the subject of the ode to other things (that are beautiful, or magnificent, etc.).

For example, you could compare your friend's eyes to the stars or your favourite food to precious gems. The most important thing to remember when you are writing an ode is that it is about your emotions. Pick something that you have a strong connection to or feel very deeply about. You will be writing about a single thing, so make sure that it's something you can open your heart about when you write.

Writing an ode is a great opportunity to allow your emotions to run wild across the page! Your passion can help you to create a beautiful poem in the form of an ode.

Laura Marie Clark

Form: Haiku

A Haiku is a three line Japanese poem that has a syllable count for each line. The syllable count for line one is five syllables, line two seven syllables, and line three has five syllables. The total syllable count for a Haiku is seventeen syllables in all. Some contemporary writers are now writing seventeen syllable run on sentences, which should not be confused with a Haiku. Haikus are technically nature based poems, and can be linked, in which case they would be linked verse Haikus.

Example:

Freedom Haiku

Cool breeze on my skin
Under the bright moonlight glow
Freedom in nature's shadow

Jody Austin

Form: Hay Na Ku

A Hay Na Ku is a Filipino Haiku. It is a contemporary word count structure developed by Eileen Tabios. It is a tercet of three lines, has a total of six words, one in the first line, two in the second line, and three in the third line. There are no restrictions on syllable counts, stressed, or rhymes. Variations include in the 'reverse' haynaku, the longest line is placed first and the shortest last. The total is still six words: three in the first line, two in the second line, and one in the third line. Multiple hay(na)ku can be chained to form a longer poem.

Example:

She Drove Black

She
Driving Black
Pushed over cattle

Profiled darkie faces
Be damned
She

Manhandled
Like savage
A disenfranchised citizen

Her young life
It mattered
See

What really happened
Sandra Bland
To

Her empty cell
It knows
Whispers

Jody Austin

Form: Tanka

A Tanka is a Japanese poem and similar to a Haiku, however it has seven lines. Tankas are nature, seasons, love, and other emotions. Line one has a five syllable count, line two is seven syllables, line three is five syllables, line four is seven syllables, and line five seven syllables. In total it has thirty one syllables. It uses simile, metaphor, and personification.

Example:

The Black Holocaust

The Black Holocaust
They say it doesn't exist
Burned bodies don't lie
DNA charred from C4
Murdered by the privileged

Eleven souls gone
The Martyrs of a movement
Forced to go back in
Black lives didn't matter then
Still don't...Thirty years later

In Memory of those murdered...
MOVE thirty years later...

Jody Austin

Form: Cinquain

A Cinquain is a five line poem. Line one is one word that is a subject or a noun. Line two is two words that are adjectives that describe line one. Line three is three words that are action verbs that relate to line one. Line four is four words, that are feelings or a complete sentence that relates to line one. Line five is one word, that is a synonym of line one or a word that sums it up.

Example:

Untitled

Staring
Upon her nape
Sifting through the shadows
Touching fears with fine fingertips
Silent

Daydreams
Broken rainbows
Searching for the sunshine
Hope is healing for two in it
Deep down

Prayers
Often answered
When it's least expected
Purposed preparation for now
Thank you

Dear God
Let them be true
These possibilities
It's time to rest this tired yin
Amen

Jody Austin

Form: Tetractys

A Tetractys poem is a five line poem that has a syllable count for each line. Line one is one syllable, line two is two syllables, line three is three syllables, line four is four syllables, and line five is ten syllables. Each line should be independent of each other and build upon each sentence. When this poem is complete it will have a nice looking pattern. The Tetractys stanzas can also be inverted upon each other.

Example:

Sweets

Sweets
Comes in
Skyscrapers
Superheroes
Tip topping towers towering on she

Touching keys tapping tingles down her spine
A symphony
Made for her
Forehead
Kisses
Him

On
Tip toes
She sees Sun
They meet half way
Moon shines light to find her star points

The best kind of heroes don't wear a cape
They just show up
Showering
Her with
Sweets

Jody Austin

Form: Etheree

Similar to the Cinquain and the Rictameter, the Etheree is a ten line structure ascending in syllable count for ten unrhymed lines. It's attributed to an American poet, Etheree Taylor Armstrong of Arkansas. An Etheree should focus on one idea or subject. Line one is one syllable, line two is two syllables, line three is three syllables, line four is four syllables, line five is five syllables, line six is six syllables, line seven is seven syllables, line eight is eight syllables, line nine is nine syllables, and line ten is ten syllables.

Example:

She Even Cries Pretty

She cries pretty in her humility
From a deep space in her modesty
She's beautiful yet does not know
Her tears are diamonds that flow
Out of unknown triumphs
Jewel in the crown
Pain muffled sounds
Not unheard
Cries are
Her

She
Will learn
Her beauty
Inside her power
Embracing herself
Loving every inch of she
Contentment in her brown skin
Confident in knowing herself
Holding herself in the highest esteem
Accepting the lineage of her strength

Look at your reflection love thine self whole
Close your eyes butterfly and soar high
Open your wings don't be afraid

Writing Tips - Volume 1

Believe in yourself fully
Gracefully as you are
This is your image
God has designed
Behold what
See you
I

Jody Austin

Form: Nonet

A nonet has nine lines. The first line has nine syllables, the second line eight syllables, the third line seven syllables, etc... until line nine that finishes with one syllable. It can be on any subject and rhyming is optional. Each line has a syllable count. Line one is one syllable, line two is two syllables, line three is three syllables, line four is four syllables, line five is five syllables, line six, is six syllables, line seven is seven syllables, line eight is eight syllables, and line nine is nine syllables.

Example:

Untitled

See
Your eyes
Speak softly
They reach inside
Touching places untouched for far too long
Dead spaces filled healing the cracks and wounds
Peeling scabs off
One by one
Until
Gone

There's
Respite
To be found
In those optics
Where the moon shines bright
Calming tsunami tides
Where the sun rises and falls
Between an oasis and Eden

Across desert sands leaving footprints
That show us how to seal the levees
That rescue the aches from the past
That stop the dams from leaking
Ceasing hearts from bleeding

Writing Tips - Volume 1

Clearing blurred vision
So we can see
To find me
Seek mine
Eyes

Jody Austin

Form: 6 Word Story

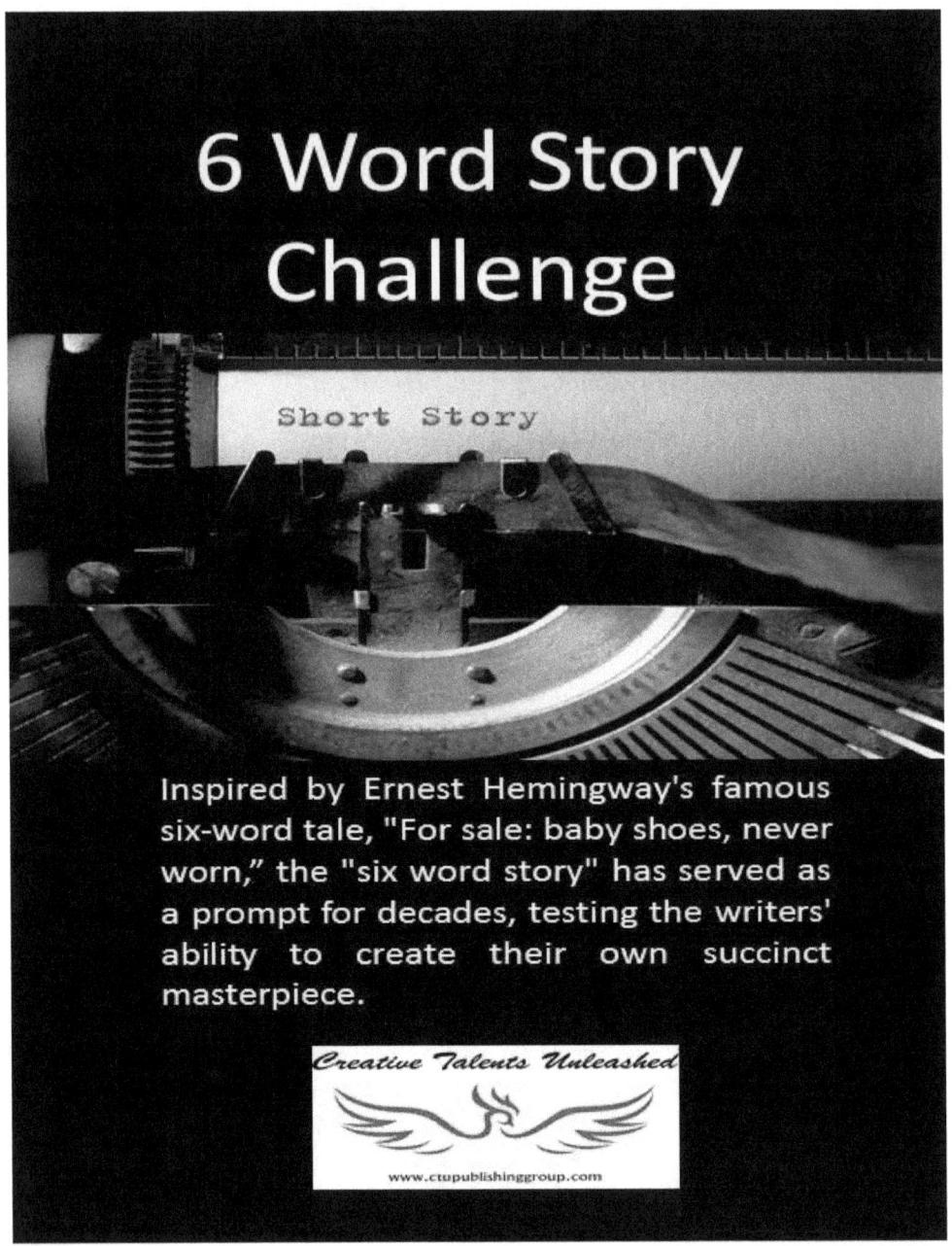

Raja Williams

Tips to Strengthen the Writer

Continuity

One of the most important things to focus on in a series of poems or chapters of a story is continuity. This means you need to think about how your first part flows into your second part, your second into your third, and so on. You could have an overarching theme or a regular time scale in order to maintain continuity.

Let's look at a few examples of how you can ensure continuity in your writing.

1. Time. Time is very important when you are writing something based on actions or events. Each section of your series could take place every day, week, month, year, ten years and so on. If your work is based around age, the seasons or a period in history then time can help you to maintain continuity.

2. Recurring characters. Regular characters allow you to build upon their personalities and can involve the audience emotionally with their struggle. Anything based on emotional or physical change could use recurring characters to keep continuity.

3. Recurring phrases. This is a clever way to link your sections together without using an especially strong connection. Similarly, recurring sentence or line structure (such as similar sentences at the beginning or end of each piece) can create a bond of continuity. These could be used in a series without any overarching character or themes, or within a series that you are writing without a strict plan.

4. Overarching theme. This does not have to be a strict theme. You could use something very focused such as a particular event, or something very flexible such as a concept. An overarching theme is a great way to link a series of poems together in one collection.

These are by no means the only ways that you can ensure continuity in your writing, of course. You will find your own ways to link to sections of your series together, but these are all good ways to maintain the flow within distinct pieces.

Laura Marie Clark

Use Active Voice

When you are writing, you can use the active or the passive voice. The active voice is a strong and direct way to say something, whereas the passive voice is usually reserved for professional and government documents. The passive voice almost sounds as though the writer is trying to avoid the subject.

Active voice places the subject of your sentence first (for example your character's name). This is followed by the action that the subject is performing (the verb), and then the object that is being affected by that verb. Passive voice is the opposite of active voice. The sentence is written in reverse order.

Examples:

Active Voice:

Sara lifted the glass.
This is the active voice. Sara is the subject. Lifting is the verb. The glass is the object that she is lifting.

Passive Voice:

The glass was lifted by Sara.
This is the passive voice. The object is first, followed by the verb, and finally the subject.

Read the example sentences aloud. You are probably more likely to speak in the active voice than in the passive voice. The passive voice removes the reader's attention from the main focus of the sentence, which should be your subject.

Laura Marie Clark

Eliminate Unnecessary Words

We have discussed using too many long or uncommon words before. It can distract your readers from your message. This time, we will discuss using unnecessary words in your writing. If you can explain something in ten words instead of thirty, then it is often better to eliminate those twenty words that you do not need.

Many writers find it difficult to write very short pieces. You need to be able to describe something, tell a story and leave a message in a small number of words, which is a difficult skill to master. There are many ways to practice cutting down your word count and removing words that are merely there to fill space and have no real significance in your piece.

In poetry, you could try rewriting an old poem but cutting the word count in half, or if you want to practice in a specific form you can try something short, like a limerick or a haiku. These will really make you think about which words you are using and why you are using them.

If you like stories, try flash fiction. There are many challenges available online, including blogs dedicated to them. These are short pieces that are usually between 100 and 200 words. There are many places where you can get tips about how to write such short stories; reading other people's stories can give you a great idea of how successful flash fiction works. You do not have to cut everything short, but neither should you use additional words for the sake of it.

Laura Marie Clark

Read Your Writing Aloud

This is particularly important when you are writing speech, but no less important for poetry and stories. Reading your writing aloud to yourself (or to other people, if you are involved in a writing group or have friends who can comment on your work) will allow you to hear what you have created in a new voice: you will be more likely to spot any errors too, as well as words and patterns that you may not have previously noticed.

When you read it out loud, the dialogue within your writing should sound like a conversation you could have in real life. By hearing it, you will be able to see where the conversation does not seem to flow correctly, where you may need to edit or which words or phrases do not seem to fit. You should also be able to hear the individual "voices" of your characters, which could help you to grow them.

Reading your poetry aloud will allow you to better understand the rhythm of your piece. You may spot something you did not notice when you were writing: a better place to break up your lines, a few words that are out of place, a section that could be expanded upon, and so on.

Your stories can also benefit from this exercise: long paragraphs or lengthy sentences will be far easier for you to spot when you are reading them out loud. Again, if one sentence does not seem to link to the next, you will be able to notice this. I often find that it is an excellent way for me to spot words that I have overused or repeated accidentally. It is a great way to develop and edit your writing.

Laura Marie Clark

Editing Your Writing

It is crucial to read through what we have written in order to review it, correct spelling or grammar mistakes, and ensure fluency. Common fixtures can include something as minor as removing repeated words or phrases or correcting tenses, and something as major as rewriting whole chapters of work. If you don't have an editor or you're just writing as a hobby, then editing can quickly become a monotonous task. It is tedious, especially so if you are used to correcting the same mistakes over and over. It can also be very daunting if you're not sure how to deal with the problem. Not everyone is a grammar expert! Going through your writing with your eyes narrowed to spot even the smallest of errors can be exhausting.

Nevertheless, there are many things that you can do in order to make editing an easier experience. If you're writing in a notebook, try typing what you've written up on a computer so that you can go through the mistakes one by one as you write, or scan them onto a machine to view them in a different light. If you're using a computer, print out what you've written and go over it with a pen or (if printing is too expensive and time consuming), change the size and font of the text before you go through it. If you're preparing a post online, preview it first on your website. By reading your creation in a different format, it should be easier for you to spot mistakes and errors that you might otherwise have missed. After all, you've probably been staring at that text for a long time.

Try not to get worked up about grammar when you're editing. If you've produced something great that really captures the attention of your audience, then a few grammar mistakes aren't going to matter. Most importantly, take your time, If you dislike editing as much as I do, then don't try to tackle massive chunks of text one after the other. You will not enjoy it.

Laura Marie Clark

The Importance of Background Research

We all like to write about things that we understand. When we do, we do not necessarily need to do massive amounts of background research: a minimal amount will do at the points in our writing where we wish to delve into the subject a little further. But usually, the more details that your writing becomes, the more likely you are to step into unknown territory.

It is not uncommon to write about something that you do not know a great deal about, however it can become obvious to your readers very quickly if you do not do the correct background research. You do not have to take a long time researching, pouring laboriously over heavy books, to learn the key points and vocabulary to slip into your writing. Many people know how to do quick but detailed research from their studies, but if you struggle then there are many places online that can help you to learn.

Avoid using websites such as Wikipedia if you can. For basic information you can use websites focused on exam revision for school students, and if you're looking for more detailed stuff, then you can bet there are websites out there that are dedicated to your subject.

Don't spend too much time on your research. You don't want to lose yourself within the research unless you're planning to dedicate an entire book to it. Perfect your skills to carry out efficient background research, then place key information within your writing to show that you have an understanding of the topic.

Laura Marie Clark

Using Images

Pictures can provide us with great inspiration as writers. It is surprising how diverse the responses to one image can be. Yet images are more than simply ways to spark our creativity and our imagination. When relevant and used in the right way, they can also complement our writing.

Inserting pictures into posts or as headers can draw attention to our writing and give the reader an impression of what they are about to read. They can also highlight a certain feature of our creation that we want people to notice, such as a house or a person, or enhance an emotion that we have written about. However, images should also be used with caution. Too many pictures can break up your piece and may distract from the flow of your writing. If you have produced a small piece of text or a poem, then it is best to have one picture at the beginning or the end of the piece that is particularly relevant to what you have written. This way, you can draw your reader in without removing their attention from the text. A long or descriptive piece of writing would be better suited to pictures between text, as they can break up the writing and give your audience a moment to pause before diving back in.

The important thing is that the images you choose are suited to whatever you have written. They can be anything from photographs to sketches. You don't have to be an artist to create something that looks good and gives off the right impression. A word of warning: be careful where you get your images from. Photographs found on Google Images can be very tempting, but sticking a copyright notice beneath the picture you have inserted in your post does not mean you have permission to use it. If you haven't got express permission from the owner, it's off limits.

Laura Marie Clark

Beginning and Ending

The beginning and ending of your writing are both equally important. They need to have an impact that draws people towards your work and leaves them feeling fulfilled, without a lot of unanswered questions. You don't need to tie everything in a neat little bow, but you don't want to leave gaping holes in your pieces either.

Your beginning needs to draw readers in and perhaps tease a little of what is going to come later on. For instance, you could have a little bit of action at the start that mimics something bigger that is going to happen, or establish the traits of your character that are going to impact their behavior. In poetry, you could insert a metaphor that you will expand upon throughout your piece: war, nature, pleasure, etc.

Your ending can have plot twists, surprises and shocks. Or it can summarize or conclude a moral lesson. It can be expected or unexpected. It can be sudden and short. If it is too punctual, however, it can leave readers with the feeling that it has not ended properly. Be careful to ensure that your ending is not too abrupt: you want it to have a positive impact on your readers (whether or not they are supposed to feel good about it). In longer poems, you could reflect or reach the end of a scene; in shorter poems, you might reach the end of your metaphor or find the exact words to describe an emotion.

There are no strict rules on how to begin or end your writing. As a writer, you may have a large number of beginnings and endings already written. Starting a piece of writing and concluding it are good skills to practice.

Laura Marie Clark

Ask For Specific Feedback

We all want feedback on our writing. Likes and comments such as "really enjoyed this, well done!" are comforting, but they are also vague. Comments that tell us what in particular someone liked or disliked about our pieces are far more helpful when we want to develop our writing skills.

Of course, we are more likely to get good feedback when we give others good feedback, and regular writers should make a habit of commenting on other people's posts when they have asked for an opinion (always be positive, be sure to mention what was good even when you give critical feedback). More importantly, if we want to know something specific about how people view our writing, then we need to ask about it. You can include a comment in your post for your readers to think about, separated from your work at either the top or the bottom of the post. You can also ask the question in a forum with a link to your work in the hope of discovering a wider audience. Wherever you choose to ask, remember to be specific: you want your readers to be focusing on the points that you wish for feedback on.

For example, don't simply say "tell me what you think" or "feedback is appreciated". Instead, ask what people think of the way you have separated your paragraphs, your use of metaphors, your punctuation or the layout of your poem.

Laura Marie Clark

Know Your Target Audience

Everything we write has a target audience. Some writers are dedicated to a particular group of people, such as young adults, and others are focused on an audience with a particular interest, such as historical fiction. Audiences can be based on age, gender, race, religion, country, social class, interest and many other things. When we write, we should think about our target audience and what they would like to read.

For example, you wouldn't include a graphic sex scene in a piece of fiction aimed at teenagers (leave that for a adult fiction!). You also don't want to include explicit language. Equally, if you're writing a poem about love, you main audience probably isn't going to be middle-aged men (though I'm sure some of you really enjoy a good love sonnet if you're perfectly honest). When you choose the language to include in your work, you need to think about what best suits your audience.

This can also apply to other sections of your writing, such as sentence structure and layout. Younger audiences may not be interesting in large blocks of writing. A poem designed to appeal to a Christian audience would be striking if it was in the shape of a crucifix. If you're really clever and you want to write about a certain country to interested lovers of travel writing, you could try to create an acrostic poem in the shape of that country. These are things that are designed to attract a certain person to your writing.

When we think about our target audience, we need to consider what will catch their eye and make them likely to read the whole of our work.

Laura Marie Clark

Blog Etiquette – Poetry & Pictures

The Internet is a wonderful thing – a place to reach anyone worldwide and share your talents, whether on social media or your own blog page. But there is a dark side to the web that many are unaware of.

You will get the usual trolls who have nothing better to do than try to start an argument, but there are also people scouring sites to steal and plagiarize your work.

I had this happen on one of my social media accounts and requested a user to remove a photo of me from his website that he used for his poetry, and he refused. I ended up blocking him from seeing my page and reported him, but since he was from an international location, there wasn't much I could do. So now on all my sites, I put a disclaimer that all my work is copyrighted and can be shared only with author credit.

On Twitter, there are many people who copy and paste writers' work and claiming it as their own. It has been an ongoing task to block these types because they can still find many ways to access your page even though you block them. This is one of the reasons I prefer to put my poetry on a picture. But you also have to be aware of the pictures you use.

I used to put my poetry on pictures from a Google search until a friend shared this article with other writers: Bloggers Beware: You CAN Get Sued For Using Pics on Your Blog – My Story by Roni Loren.

Roni was one of the unfortunate few who was unaware of photography copyright laws and learned the hard way about using unauthorized pictures on her blog. She lists quite a few points on what she learned about Fair Use:

It DOESN'T MATTER...

- if you link back to the source and list the photographer's name
- if the picture is not full-sized (only thumbnail size is okay)
- if you did it innocently
- if your site is non-commercial and you made no money from the use of the photo
- if you didn't claim the photo was yours
- if you've added commentary in addition to having the pic in the post
- if the picture is embedded and not saved on your server
- if you have a disclaimer on your site.
- if you immediately take down a pic if someone sends you a DMCA notice (you do have to take it down, but it doesn't absolve you.)

Thanks to Roni's experience, I decided the safest way to share my poems is by using my own photos. I have a few cameras in my house so I started putting them to good use. I searched how to create a DIY light-box studio, set it up on a table and choose random objects to shoot like pens, seashells, flowers etc. I have also been practicing using Photoshop with the special effects feature to create more variety with my photos. I even send templates of my own photos to my phone for those impromptu writing moments and then use the Photgrid app to post my poetry.

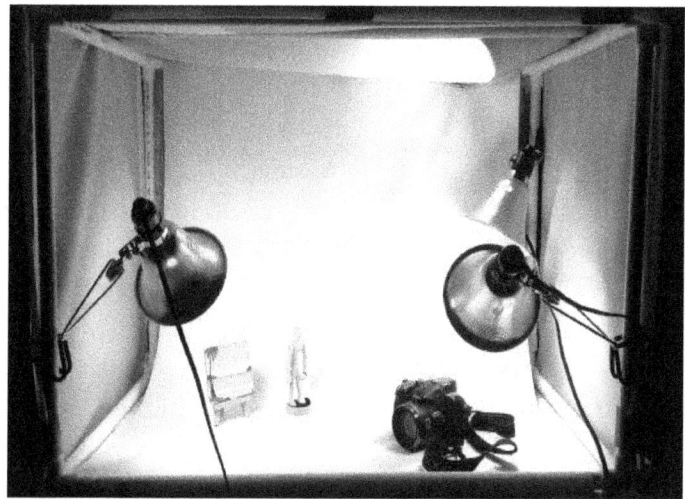

Just because a photo, a font, or even a logo from the web says "free to use" doesn't always mean it is. Research the website it was on and read all the fine print about terms of use to be sure. There are many sites where you can pay fees or also purchase to use photos:

Corbis Images

Creative Market

iStock

Shutterstock

If you can't afford to splurge, just take your own photos to be safe. Most smart phones take high quality pictures so put them to good use during your daily travels. Keep an eye out for: interesting textures on a wall, an unusual tree or funny shaped clouds in the sky. Open your eyes to the world and use it at no charge.

Just remember – not everyone is respectful to the original work shared on the web, but as writers, photographers and artists, we should all extend that courtesy to those in our own community.

Donna J. Sanders

Raise Your Voice

Since social media has blossomed, it has been a playground for the narcissists of today. Some will post a selfie daily – sometimes more than once a day even – awaiting a plethora of approvals from their friends to boost their ego. There are those who want recognition for the good deeds they do, rather than be humble about it. We poets, we do it too. Writing about ourselves, our problems, and our pain; masking the self-centeredness by sometimes using a third person perspective.

There's absolutely nothing wrong writing about our emotions. It is how most of us cope with toils of reality. But we are writers for a reason. We have been given a gift to speak for the entire world to hear but sometimes our audience wants to hear a bit more. They read about the woes of depression, addiction and broken hearts, and can certainly relate to our words because they are human too. What if we were to expand our minds and speak for groups amidst humanity? For the trafficked children who can't be heard. For the souls of those in other countries who don't have the same rights as we do. For the endangered animals depleting in supply. Even for the forests or food supply getting scarcer daily. Many writers are afraid to get political these days for the fear of offending someone. But if we don't address the subjects others are afraid to talk about, who is left to say something?

Poet Langston Hughes touched on the delicate subject of slavery in many of his poems. In "The Negro Mother," the narrator speaks of her struggles as a slave and the hardships endured while dreaming of the day slaves would be free. She encourages her children to make a better future and not forget the reason she persevered. The poem speaks for all slaves who have been mistreated and fought for their freedom.

The world has not been free of slavery even though many have fought long and hard for civil rights. There are countries where citizens are slaves to corrupt governments and militias. There are many companies who treat their employees like laborers beneath them. Many in society have become hostages to the drug companies and doctors shoving medication down our throats, when they can't figure out how to fix the actual problem. Slavery is a cause far and wide with much to write about and by putting these issues in our poetry, we can bring awareness to the injustices of the world.

CTU's very own Sue Lobo decided to dedicate an entire book of poems to the animals she loves dearly. Sue was fortunate enough to live in Africa, getting a first-hand look at the massacre of the country's beloved animals. Every poem in her book Wild Whisperings is written about animals; some from the perspective of the creatures we share the planet with. It is such a passionate cause for her, that all the proceeds from the book goes to Save The Rhino International Fund.

So if you are you a nature activist, a strict vegetarian, or protest the use of animal testing, these are causes that could use a voice in poetry. Write to inform about the lands around us being destroyed. Educated others about the poisons in our food and why eating naturally is beneficial. Make people aware of the companies still being cruel to animals for the sake of research and development. Give nature its due because our plants, trees and animals cannot speak for themselves.

When you decide to touch on delicate subjects, be ready for those who are waiting to pounce and argue the cause. They are out there and they are entitled to their opinions just as you are. But as the world continues to be divided day by day with so many different points of views, think about how you will respond. Do you want to drag out an argument with someone who has nothing better to do, as it could go on and on forever? Take all comments about your work as constructive criticism and tread cautiously. Don't take away from the intent of the subject you are writing about. Sometimes you just have to play nice with the few who bring negativity and move along.

Don't feel confined in your writing because of how the rest of the world will react. You have a voice for a reason. Raise it. Give it depth so your audience will stay interested. You never know who may need to hear what you have to say.

Donna J. Sanders

Social Media: Personal vs. Professional Pages

When you make the decision to step into the writing world, it is wise to make some safe and smart decisions when using social media. Some prefer to share everything publicly on a personal page. Others might prefer keeping their private life separate from their professional one. If you plan on sharing your writing with the rest of the world, then I suggest the latter.

On Facebook, I cannot tell you how many friend requests I get from fellow writers on my personal page because of posting my poetry in other community pages. Though I really adore my writing family, some of these people are total strangers and I would rather not give them access to my personal life. I share some very intimate moments with my family and friends, and I'd rather not let people I am unfamiliar with browse through all my posts and photos. The world is full of horrible people who can easily manipulate their way into your life for the wrong reasons, and I would rather not take that chance.

Social media sites have made it very easy to create professional pages for an author, even letting you use a pseudonym if you want to remain anonymous or get creative. I created two pages of my own on FB; one to share my poetry and another to share poetry from other writers. My Twitter, Instagram, and Google+ pages are strictly for anything poetry related and links to my blog articles.

Here are some other Creative Talents Unleashed authors who have use social media to promote their work. Explore their sites to get ideas on how to maintain a professional page.

- Adam Brown – Twitter: https://twitter.com/adamlevonbrown
- Billy Charles Root – Tumblr: http://wcroot75.tumblr.com/
- Christopher Allen Breidinger – Facebook: https://www.facebook.com/PoetChristopher
- Damon E. Johnson – Twitter: https://twitter.com/damonej28
- Debra McLain – Facebook: https://www.facebook.com/DKMcLain
- Demitri Tyler – Twitter: https://twitter.com/Author_Tyler
- Lindsey F. Rhodes – Twitter: https://twitter.com/LFRII76
- Nolan P. Holloway Jr. – Twitter: https://twitter.com/nolanpholloway
- Raja Williams – Facebook: https://www.facebook.com/RajasInsight
- Tony Haynes – Facebook: https://www.facebook.com/tonyhaynes.selfhelppoetry

There are also many sites like www.blogger.com and www.wordpress.com to create your own blog page at no cost. With the resources we have today, it is much easier for a writer to share his/her work. But be aware of sharing photos and the work of others on a blog, because the rules are a bit different.

Ref: https://theraven6825.wordpress.com/2015/09/06/blog-etiquette-poetry-pictures/

Some writers also tend to worry about sharing on such a vast scale. In the United States, any written work is protected under copyright laws, but it wouldn't hurt to put a disclaimer on your page or with your writing to make it clear.

Read more about copyright here:

http://fairuse.stanford.edu/overview/faqs/copyright-protection/

It can be a little frightening when you get involved in the world of writing. There are people out there who will blatantly steal another artist's work and post it as their own. Sometimes there is not much you can do if it occurs in another country or the person has concealed their identity. Don't be discouraged though – just make sure you protect yourself and your work as best as you can.

Donna J. Sanders

Handling Rejection

In life, we sometimes have to deal with rejection. The same happens, at one point or another, to most people who attempt to publish their writing. Whether you want to be a professional writers or you're just curious and want to get better, at some point you will probably consider submitting something you have written to a blog, journal, or other publication. You might want a little more attention or you might want to see your name in lights – whatever your reasons, you need to be able to continue writing and submitting if you are rejected.

Rejection does not mean that your writing is poor. The publisher may not be looking for something within that genre at that time. If you're in a competition, there may be such a high standard of writing from everybody that you simply did not get chosen. It is important that you are able to motivate yourself to continue building up your skills and do not allow this rejection to prevent you from writing.

There are many ways to handle rejection, and many websites that can advise you on the best ways to deal with it in various situations. As a writer, you must find the way that you can overcome your rejection. You could submit to other publications – the more you try, the more likely you are to succeed. Motivate yourself to keep writing: remember that there are many famous authors who have been rejected. One setback is not enough to judge your skills on – and keep telling yourself that until you taste success!

Laura Marie Clark

Give A Book

Every year, the shopping crowds get crazier for those Black Friday and holiday deals. Parents fight for the most expensive and trendiest toys for their children who end up destroying them in a few months. Some people buy gifts just for the sake of giving, without really putting their hearts into it. But there is one gift that will never go out of style – books!

It doesn't matter the occasion, books are fundamental. At some point or another one has crossed our path. There are books for all ages and on so many topics, it is probably easier than you think to pick the right one for whoever you are shopping for.

For the little ones: there are colorful pop-up books, quite a few with textures for baby to touch and feel, and so many delicate stories to keep a toddler entertained.

Young adults can be a very finicky bunch, but there are more than enough books to match their personalities. Dystopian stories like The Hunger Games and The Fifth Wave series seem to be a trend among many right now. Some may be into the arts and there are numerous books about music, acting, and fashion for that creative bunch. Those who love cosplay and gaming would probably enjoy the comic books being turned into blockbuster movies. And for those teens who are struggling to find themselves, there are lists of books tackling the social issues they usually don't feel comfortable discussing with most adults.

Adult books are bountiful, but how does one chose the right book for a friend, co-worker or relative they hardly know? If that person you are shopping for seems a little stressed and maybe has a creative side, buy them an adult coloring book with a box of colored pencils or markers. This trend has been ongoing for those who just need some down time or to spend some fun moments with their kids. If that co-worker is constantly talking about their favorite celebrity or really into politics, there are many biographies and memoirs they might appreciate. If you have a friend always posting about food on social media, there are so many cookbooks, books about kitchen appliances, and a few food parodies for those who are obsessed with anything culinary.

Here at Creative Talents Unleashed, we have a poetry lover's dream. If you know someone who loves to read or write poetry, then a book from one of our authors would make a fine gift. Here are a few to choose from:

Off the Leash by Ryan Vallee

Don't open this book and expect to see the normal. This is your warning. I'm different, but I'm real. I spell things out in a semi-clever way. I'm not the best, I'll never be the best. I'll never win an award. But if I win your hearts, I'll have accomplished all I need. Feel me. That's all I ask.

City of the World by Laura Clark

These poems tell my story. They are the high points and the low points. They are the memories that I gleefully recall to my friends. Some of them were written when I was in Ho Chi Minh City; the rest can only attempt to recall the mixture of emotions that my memories conjoure within me. Through these poems, I take you from the beginning of my adventure to the end, ten months later, when I returned to England to begin the next part of my life.

A Treasure of Seashells by Anne D. Salyer

I wish I could remember how the words started. I only have a vague memory of sitting in my garden. I have never been good at expressing myself but the words came. I was encouraged to breath them by someone who didn't really exist. Now that non-existent person and I no longer speak but the words are still there. If you are reading them, thank you for your indulgence. Like a neglectful mother I give birth to them and then send them out into the world. Please treat them gently

Even if you have already finished shopping or have no one to really buy a present for, it doesn't hurt to buy a book and give it to complete stranger or donate one to a library. A book is a gift that keeps on giving. So buy one for yourself and absorb some knowledge or be engulfed in an epic adventure. Books are the elixir of life, and to taste them is to nourish ourselves with wisdom.

Donna J. Sanders

After You're Published – What Happens Next?

After You're Published – What Happens Next?

Becoming a published author is an exciting time. You have spent weeks, months, or even years writing, and creating your books manuscript. You have invested a piece of you into the words, the lines, and the total outcome. Each step of the way the excitement builds. From the moment you submit your manuscript, to the acceptance, to your first view of what will soon be your book, and then choosing your cover. All high points of the progression from the first thought "I want to publish a book."

You are on your way . . . and will soon join the literary circle of people that can say "I am an Author."

The excitement of saying "I am an Author" is the most wonderful feeling of accomplishment, next to actually holding your book in your hands for the first time. I'll never forget the day my package came in the mail. I remember cutting the tape, unfolding the flaps, and catching the first glimpse of my words in print. It is a feeling that I will never forget.

But, what happens next?

Unless you have PAID a Marketing Team to market your book, your journey as an author lays in your own hands. It is up to you, who hears and sees that you have a book available for purchase. Most new authors, don't realize that they just took on a new job. It is now your "job" to represent yourself as an author.

Those who are dedicated to their new job as an author, will sell books. Those that sit back and say "I published a book, I am an author", but have no actions behind the words will not sell books and will only have the gratification of saying "I am an author" but will not reap the rewards.

The actions you take to represent yourself will determine your success.
 Don't be afraid to put yourself out there!
 Share your story!

You worked hard at creating your story, you obtained a publisher or self-published, and you have a book that readers are waiting to hear about. Now it's time to get busy Marketing Yourself!

Here are some Marketing Suggestions to help you reach more people:

• Create an Announcement that your book is Now Available
• Take a picture of yourself holding your book and write a quote about it "Share It"
• Share excerpts of your work frequently on social media sites
• Create an Author Page or Start a Blog
• Explore new social media outlets you are not currently using
• Read an excerpt on a Radio Show – Opportunities 7 days a week
• Set up a book signing – Your own hosted event or public library event.
• Check to see if your local newspaper can write an article about your book
• Perform at "Live events"
• Set up Promotions or giveaways of your book
• Participate in Book Review Programs
• Join Writing Groups

As you can see, all of our suggestions require you to be actively connecting with people. The more people you connect with, the more opportunities you will have. Don't give up, the work is hard, but those that stay the course and have an action plan, eventually create their own success. Nothing happens overnight, but with dedication and determination you can become a top selling author.

Just Remember . . . Your Author Journey Lays In Your Own Hands!

Raja Williams

The Obstacles We Face as Writers

When I had a full-time job and taking care of my husband – who was injured on the job two years ago and is still suffering from his injures, including a traumatic brain injury – finding the time to write was my number one struggle. I would often jot my ideas on breaks or stay up a little later at night to write down my thoughts. But it wasn't enough to keep up with all the emotions I had to deal with every day.

Writing poetry has always been therapy for me. Instead of indulging in foods or drinks to drown my sorrows, I often have to cry it out and then write. I would wake up the next day refreshed and ready to go.

When I became unemployed nine months ago, writing took a different turn. Life slowed down and I was able to sit back and take in everything I was missing. I noticed the changes in nature more; from the flowers blooming in the spring, to the storms brewing in the Florida skies. I paid attention to all going on in the world: the people suffering from tragedy and war, destruction of historic places, and the treasures discovered once hidden beneath. Since my husband's injury, I am educated on the unjust laws passed, the truth about the way doctors operate, and what people with TBI and PTSD have to deal with.

These experiences have made it easier to be inspired to write and I have written more than enough to publish several books, but the next struggle is to market my work to a very competitive audience in a genre that many feel to hold no future financially. And with no income at the moment, it has been even harder to use the resources available to promote myself.
Making a living by writing would be a dream for me, but it is not the reason why I do it. I hesitated for many, many years to share my writing with anyone,

but I felt I needed to do so. I have touched more than one life with some of my poems, and that is why I continue to write. And I will keep writing and publishing books until I have exhausted all that I have to give.

Damon E. Johnson, The Vineyard: Exploding Grapes.

One of the major challenges I face as a writer is trying to find time and creative space to just write on a consistent basis. The everyday hustle with work and family does not leave me with much opportunity to get heavy involved with writing. Indeed I write every day. But if I have the time, I don't have the creative space. And if I have the creative space, I don't have the time. Creative space is that place you go where you can relax and let your pen flow uninterrupted. I haven't been there in a while. I feel I haven't written my best work yet. Maybe the Holidays will provide a change. But until I can find a happy medium, I will continue to write in the creative space I often find in my head…

Sue Lobo, Wild Whisperings.

My biggest problem as a writer is that I live in Spain. Spain is a country that does not rate high in their reading habits & much less poetry which is my genre. Although I am fluent in Spanish being married to a Spaniard & having lived here for over 40 years, I only write in English because that´s how I think & where my inspiration stems from, my mother tongue. Online one may publish a book perfectly but when it comes to marketing & selling, I hit serious problems. I often feel like moving to the UK or the U.S.A. because I think I would have a better chance at selling my work in those places than I do here. I do approach the local authorities like the city councils, libraries, English speaking groups etc…. but they show such little interest because they do not understand what it is all about. Maybe I should learn to write in Spanish, believe me I have tried & have even come fourth in a poetry competition in Spain, but I have no inspiration whatsoever in this area so it does no work at all.

Time and location are the obstacles for Damon and Sue. Having a family can certainly limit the time one has to write. Being a parent is a full time job, and you also have to give some time to that significant other in your life while carrying out those every day chores. Sue's problem is a most unique one. She lives in a country where poetry is not very popular, which makes it even harder to get recognized. At CTU, we are most thankful that her path crossed with ours and we are able to share her work with the American audience.

Some writers just take it day by day, like Nolan Holloway. Perhaps we can try his method – just live in the moment and let the ideas flow when they need to…

Nolan P. Holloway Jr., Journey to the Poetic Light "Illuminations".

Life drives my writing. My moods, music and events of the day fuel my mind to scribe. I think and sometimes dream in poetic images. When the inspiration does not come, I don't worry because just living will bring the blessings of my next scribe. It is that simple for me.

These are some of the reasons why it is so important to support a writer's work. Their peers are struggling themselves so it can be hard for another writer to buy books from a fellow author. We often have to rely on word of mouth through social media to get our names out there. Not all of us are lucky enough to have a celebrity endorsement to gain recognition.

Donna J. Sanders

Choosing The Right Poems For Publishing

Within the top ten poetry books on Amazon are: Where the Sidewalk Ends by Shel Silverstein, Edgar Allan Poe's Complete Tales and Poems, Milk and Honey by Rupi Kaur and Chasers of the Light by Tyler Knott Gregson. Each book is unique in its theme. One is fun and witty, meant for the eyes of the young. The other delves into the macabre darkness within. A third takes a journey into the author's life. And the last one gives readers a glimpse of hope.

Most poets strive to have a book published because we know others share the same thoughts, have been through similar struggles, and hope that by taking the risk of revealing our words to the public, that those who don't know how to cope with life will see some glimmer of hope in our poetry. Some of us have been writing at a very young age and have gathered quite a collection of poems. We have seen how our writing has evolved over time. But when it is time to submit a collection for publishing, it becomes a difficult choice.

No one can really tell you what the right choices are when picking poems for a book, or what will be successful. It is a very difficult and competitive market unless you have a large following or a major publishing company willing to spend the money to promote you. But most poets don't do it for the fame or money. We write because we enjoy it.

So when an opportunity comes to submit a manuscript, perhaps do some research or just use your heart to decide which poems to submit. Go back to your social media pages or blog and see which poems obtained the most feedback. Scour the top poetry book lists and see which themes are remaining steady. Or take this as the opportunity to try something no other poet has done before, and be an original.

You don't always have to give the world what it needs; sometimes you may need to share the right poems for yourself. If you lived a life filled with abuse, maybe sharing your poems can be your therapy and feel fulfillment knowing it may reach out to someone else. If you have experienced being in a desperate financial situation, share your story and how you survived, as many out there might need those poems of encouragement. If you are fighting for a cause, use your poetry to bring awareness to it.

If you are ready to get your poems out there, I suggest taking advantage of any opportunities available.

Creative Talents Unleashed is offering a 5-year poetry publishing contract to one lucky winner. This is a chance of a lifetime because not a lot of contests are out there that allow you to submit without a fee. All you have to do is submit a sample manuscript with ten poems to get started.

Donna J. Sanders

Anthologies – Should I or Shouldn't I Submit My Work?

With the rise of self-publishing abilities we are seeing a significant rise in anthology publishing offers and opportunities. Often writers are sought out in writing groups on facebook and other social networks and are invited to participate. Most often, writers are honored that they have been asked to include their work, and will instantly say "Yes, I'd love to", or "I would be honored to have my work included" without taking the time to first investigate the offer.

Sadly, in most cases the writer has agreed to participate in something they know little about, all they know is their work is going to be published. No questions were asked, work was simply chosen, sent, and then the writer just waits for the outcome.

Most writers don't take the time to think about how their work will be represented. Who will be collecting the revenue for their contribution, and the biggest question; is the publication even worthy of publishing?

Here are a list of questions you as a writer should be asking:

1. *Who is publishing the book?*
2. *Have they published before?*
3. *Who will earn the royalties for said book?*
4. *How much will the book be sold for?*
5. *How will the book be distributed?*
6. *How will the book be marketed?*

These are just the basic questions that every writer offered a place in an

Anthology should ask. As a writer myself, I make sure to do my due diligence and I take it even a step further because once you have been published in the book, you can't take it back if it turns out to not be a good deal or a shady publishing. You will always be connected to that publishing, it will represent you whether you like it or not.

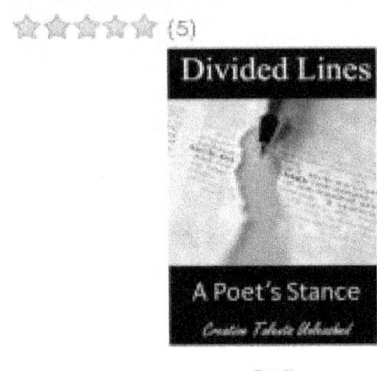

I instantly go to Amazon and research other anthologies offered by the person representing the anthology. I purchase a book from them if they have already published. By purchasing one of their previous publishing's you can personally see how well their books are put together. You can also utilize the "Look Inside" option on Amazon to view a select few pages of one of their publishing's. I personally, don't recommend publishing with anyone whom has never published before.

Far too often, writers are not doing their due diligence and are just saying yes! This past year alone, I have seen at least ten people I am friends with announce on social media "I am so honored to have been included in this anthology" and post a link for friends and family to purchase the book. When I viewed the books, I was appalled that they felt honored to be in a book so poorly put together, or priced beyond the reach of most readers. Who publishes a book of 49 to 80 pages and asks $59.00 for it? Better question is, who is going to buy it at that cost? And whom is collecting said monies?

We, at Creative Talents Unleashed offer anthology publications several times a year. We do not charge an entry fee, or reading fee, and we present quality publications every time we publish. 100 % of our anthology royalties earned are donated to the "Starving Artist Fund" which enables writers to become published authors at zero cost to the writer. Our Three Anthologies, Love, A Four Letter Word, Unleashed, and Divided Lines brought in enough revenue for us to offer Six Authors Full Publishing Scholarships this year. Divided Lines alone, brought in nearly $500 revenue in its opening release month. I bring the details of this anthology royalty to your attention because I want you to recognize the kind of money that can be made off your work. Make sure that if you participate in an anthology that the funds aren't being collected and kept by one person. They should be distributed, or used to assist other writers or publications. If this is not the case, and you decide to participate anyway, then know that someone else is banking on your hard work!

In short, make sure you aren't the author that is embarrassed to have participated in a publication, simply do your homework, investigate, and know what you are getting into before you simply say "Yes!"

Raja Williams

When is the Best Time for an Author to Release a Second or Third Book?

Have you entertained the thought of publishing another book? Are you questioning when the best time to release a book is? Rest assured, it's not a guessing game. For the serious author; those that write and market themselves and their books, the best time to create a manuscript for publication is right now, in the heat of an August summer!

It's time to start thinking holiday gift-buying season already! Books make great gifts, but will yours be ready? Holiday Shopping is usually the highest time of the fiscal year for authors that are presenting themselves and the books they have written. Are you ready to utilize the upcoming shopping season?

If you plan on marketing for this upcoming holiday season, you should plan for a Mid-November book release. Which means as of right now, you have a three month window to finish your manuscript, edit, design, and publish your new book.

Often a second or third book release will also stimulate sales of previous books; boosting your ratings on amazon and creating buzz. Remember . . . people love referrals. We love hearing how someone else felt about a product or service. It encourages us to feel; we too want that item or service. Regardless if you are releasing a second or third book, any author, at any time can choose to market for success.

Raja Williams

I Asked a Friend to Write My Books Foreword

Think of a Foreword like this...

Your foreword is like the commercial for your book.

If people are drawn in by the foreword, they consider looking further at your writing and may purchase your book.

When you read your foreword for the first time . . . You should say "YES!"

Yes, the writer of your Foreword captured the essence of the contents within your book and vividly told the reader what to expect!

If you don't strongly resonate with your commercial, you need a re-write, or to get a new writer!

Don't allow "Feelings" to get in the way. Your book after all, is a product.

Raja Williams

I Dedicate This Book To…

The meat of your book is now complete. Now it is time to add a few garnishes in the beginning and at the end. You ponder who you would like to dedicate your book to. It is a most difficult task trying to figure out who should be acknowledged on this page.

From No Thanks by E.E. Cummings

It could be the names of close family and friends. It could be a group of people or a cause you support. It could even be your worst enemy. Some authors have included conversations with others or a short amusing snippet. Author E.E. Cummings even went as far as thanking the 14 publishers who rejected his poetry manuscript and titled the collection No Thanks. Even more amusing, he made the list of their names into the shape of an urn.

Don't let this part of the process stress you out. Take some time to really think about it. You can get as creative as you want or keep it simple.

The next time you read a book, don't skip out on reading the dedication page, as it can sometimes be a very entertaining read. Below are some of the most unique dedications from some very famous authors:

Charles Bukowski, Post Office – 1971

This is presented as a work of fiction and dedicated to nobody

Hugh Howey, Wool – 2011

For those brave enough to hope

Mark Twain, Adventures of Huckleberry Finn – 1985

Persons attempting to find a motive in this narrative will be prosecuted; persons attempting to find a moral in it will be banished; persons attempting to find a plot in it will be shot.

BY ORDER OF THE AUTHOR.

Donna J. Sanders

Marketing Yourself – Don't Leave Out Important Information

I was recently chatting with an author whom compared his marketing techniques as being just the same or better than that of another author whom was seeing more success. The author I was speaking with felt that his work was just as good, and he worked just as hard at presenting himself so he was questioning why the other author was seeing more success. Why was the other author receiving more likes, comments, shares, and sales he asked? Stating that he shares and promotes his work regularly, he engages with his commenters, and tells people about his book. I was silent for a moment, as I was mentally processing and evaluating both authors marketing techniques and approaches.

In my moment of silence the author said "My writing isn't good is it? Just be honest, tell me!" It wasn't that his work was not good, in fact; he is an amazing writer. Both authors, presented wonderful books that deserve to be read by the masses. Since he was asking for the feedback, I assured him I adored his writing; which I do, and that I wanted to give honest feedback and to do that I would review his marketing techniques, and that of the compared author and get back to him the following day with some critique and feedback.

Here is what I found. Both authors shared at least twice a week a piece from their book on their main social media pages. Both authors are also sharing their work in writing groups found on facebook. Both authors were sharing reviews, pictures, or sales info at least once a week on facebook and twitter. Both authors are utilizing different platforms such as community forums like "A Shared Format 4 Poets" or sites like Goodreads, using different sales techniques on a regular basis.

So what set these equally talented poets apart?

"MISSING INFORMATION – OR LACK OF INFORMATION"

Writing Tips - Volume 1

We are living in a time where information is at our fingertips. Everything is just one click away. In this fast paced time we reside in, if you have not provided all the details, you are forgotten as fast as you were read. If your link is not clickable and present in the post, chances are your reader just moved on. We are curious, spontaneous people, and if there is more info presented to us in that moment of reading we are more inclined to "Click" for further information.

The author asked why I'm not capturing sales, likes, comments and shares, when he worked just as hard as other authors? Through observing his marketing techniques I found he was not providing the information the reader needed to take it to the next level.

Was he marketing himself?

Yes, he was.

But he was half-ass marketing himself, leaving out the most important part of the post; the link to get more information.

Here is an example of the marketing difference:

Facebook Author Post: (Questioning Author) Family and Supporters – My poetry book is available free this weekend, you can find it by the title on amazon.com Thank you for the support.

Note: No Link Provided, No Title of Book Provided. The author is asking you to go to amazon and search for the book if you really want it.

Facebook Author Post: (Compared Author) To say thank you for all the love and support of my poetry you have shown me, I am giving away by book free this weekend. Please take me up on my free offer and download your copy today. Thank you. * Link Attached to post.

Note: The link and picture of his book is clearly shown and is one "Click" away from the reader downloading. He not only thanks his readers but asks them to please take him up on his free offer.

EXAMPLE OF HOW AN EFFECTIVE MARKETING CAMPAIGN SHOULD LOOK

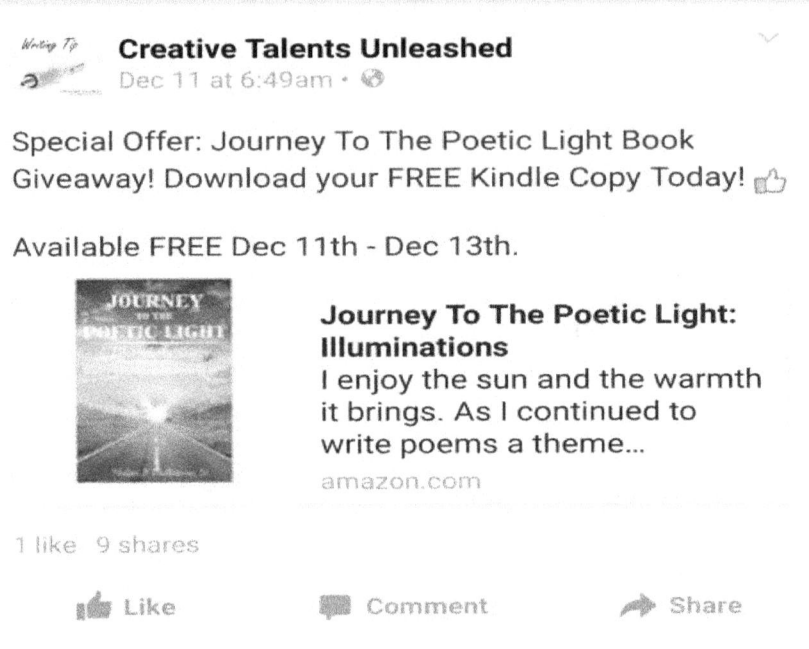

Far too often great writers share their work but fail to give the reader the option to look further at their work and possibly purchase it. As stated previously, we as people will look at more info if it is already provided to us. But if we have to go search for it, and we don't have good enough reason to go searching, we simply move on to the next thing we want to look at, therefore good authors are missing out on selling their books for the lack of information they provide in original post.

If you are asking your readers to check out your new website, there has to be a "Clickable" link within the post, or you are wasting your time and effort.

If you are promoting a new book, you have to have a "Clickable" link within the post or you are losing possible sales.

What most writers don't realize is, the moment that you decided to become a published author, you became an entrepreneur, and it's now your job to represent yourself. So make sure that you don't half-ass market yourself and take full advantage of technology, and offer smooth, professional, "Clickable" marketing campaigns.

Just Remember . . . Your Author Journey Lays In Your Own Hands! Make sure you are providing all the necessary information to market yourself efficiently.

Raja Williams

Why a Book Review is Important

Last year, Amazon decided to open its first physical bookstore in Seattle. One of the criteria for the books to be sold in the store is that it must be rated 4 stars or above. The chosen books are displayed with the online rating and customer review. Hence, why writing a book review is so important.

This is not just an incentive for writers, but for those who read books as well. If you support any writer, a book review can be one of the most rewarding gifts you can give, besides purchasing their book. When I purchase any item online, I make sure to look at the reviews for the products before I make a final decision. Even when searching for recipes, I read the comments to find out if the recipe was a hit or what ingredients were used to modify to make it better.

If someone asks for a review of their book, don't cringe because you feel you're writing skills are not that good. A review doesn't have to be professionally scribed. It is just your opinion of the work you purchased. It doesn't have to be lengthy either. A few short lines will be appreciated by any writer.

Here are a few questions to consider and suggestions to assist when writing a poetry book review:

Writing Tips - Volume 1

- Does the title of the book align with the contents?

  Perhaps find a poem in the book that coincides with the title and give some insight about the poem.

- What do you think of the poet from the foreword or info about the author?

  Delve into why you think the poet writes about a certain genre or what they were inspired by.

- What is the author's intention?

  Pick a few poems and suggest who you think the poet is writing for. The book could be a self-journey or reaching out to a specific group of people.

You can choose a favorite line from a poem and explain why you like it and use it as a simple review. If you want to get a little more technical, do a comparison of the contents if the poet has more than one book. You can write as little or as much as you want. What is most important is that you take some time to let a writer know their work was read. It is a small task that will be appreciated very much.

Donna J. Sanders

Reasons Why You should Join a Writing Group

Whether you are new to writing or a seasoned professional, a writer's group is a great resource to help you hone your writing skills, sound out your wild and crazy ideas, and find true support amongst other individuals.

A good writing group can offer you the following:

1. Information: You can receive tips, news about upcoming publications and contests, workshops, retreats, and other valuable information from your writing peers.

2. Inspiration: Group members can be an amazing source for new ideas and inspiration.

3. Evaluation: A good writing group will have members that offer constructive critique that can assist you in gaging how your writing is being perceived and read. * Don't be afraid to ask for critique!

4. Education: You can learn different writing techniques from reading other writers work.

5. Promotion: Sharing your work in a writing group helps promote your work and reach more readers. If you are a member of an interactive writing group there is a strong commitment to community where members both share and read one another's work.

6. Socialization: As writers we enjoy the benefit of sharing, collaborating with other writers, and forming friendships with other like-minded people.

So what are you waiting for? Join a writing group today and get inspired, motivated, and helpful feedback from other like-minded writers.

Writing Groups by Creative Talents Unleashed:

The Writers Connection

– A community resource for writers to share any and all work pertaining to writing. Here you will find Poetry, Book Excerpts, Book Promotions, Q & A's, Events, and more.

www.facebook.com/groups/WritersConnection

Creative Talents Unleashed "Writers Group"

– We are a core family of writers striving to make an impact with the words we share. We are here to uplift and support one another in our writing endeavors. All members of this group agree to participate and interact with one another. Strict Guidelines Apply to assure a great writing experience within this group.

www.facebook.com/groups/ctupublishing

Raja Williams

Epilogue

About the Author

Donna J. Sanders

Donna is a freelance writer and blogger in West Palm Beach, FL. She is the author of Ataraxia – a poetry collection about the struggles we face, the state of the world and how to see beauty in the simplest things, and Cardboard Signs – poems to bring awareness about homelessness, mental illness, self-esteem and the injustices many face.

Donna's Links

https://theraven6825.wordpress.com/

www.facebook.com/DonnaJSanders6825

www.ctupublishinggroup.com/donna-j.-sanders.html

About the Author

Jody Austin

My poetry styles are versatile in which I enjoy bringing a positive message. I participate in open mics and poetry/spoken word events as often as I can.

'This Is My Pen Vol 1.' my Poetry/Spoken Word CD debuted October 4th 2013 and is being released in print in 2016. I am in the studio working on my second poetry compilation and published chapbook projects. I am the Co-Administrator/Co-Founder of Family Poetry Collective (Philadelphia based poetry group) & the Co-Founder of 'The Collective' Open Mic Poetry & All Artist Open Mic Night Show.

Jody's Link

www.ctupublishinggroup.com/jody-austin-.html

About the Author

Laura Marie Clark

Laura is a 23 year old English woman with a history degree residing in the UK. She has been writing for many years and enjoys writing horror/fantasy stories, as well as poetry. Laura released her first poetry book "City Of The World" in November of 2015.

Laura's Links

www.ctupublishinggroup.com/laura-marie-clark.html

https://inspiredstoriesandpoems.wordpress.com/

About the Author

Raja Williams

Ms. Raja Williams, also known as Raja's Insight fiercely arrived on the writer's scene in 2012 after being awakened by a world renounced poet and song writer whom encouraged her to write daily. After nearly twenty years of pent up words only floating in her own head she began to allow the words to spill out onto empty pages and find way to readers that needed encouraging words. Raja entered one of her poems into a poetry contest in 2013 and won a full publishing contract and released her first book "The Journey Along The Way" in January of 2014 with Inner Child Press.

Through the publishing process and having connected with so many amazing writers and poets from around the world Raja was moved to create a community for writers known as "Creative Talents Unleashed."

Raja's Links

www.ctupublishinggroup.com/raja-williams-.html

www.facebook.com/RajasInsight

www.RajasInsight.com

Publishing Assistance

Starving Artist

In 2013 after publishing her own book, Ms. Raja Williams quickly realized that there were many writer's throughout the world needing assistance in getting published. Her writing peers were reaching out to her asking for assistance and guidance in getting their own work published. Many of the writers were from other countries indicating that even accessing the World Wide Web was a challenge for them, never mind trying to find a publisher to assist them. Financial hardships were also preventing writers from sharing their beautiful poetry and words of wisdom.

Right away Raja felt inclined to assist her writing peers so she established the "Starving Artist Fund." A fund that will assist writers that are ready to submit their manuscript and become published authors at either a discounted rate or a full publishing scholarship. In 2014 Raja published our first book "Love, A Four Letter Word" with the help from 28 poets from around the world that donated their work to the publishing of said book to help establish the startup fund. All proceeds from our sales from all anthology books are being donated to the Starving Artist Fund.

For More Information Please Visit Our Website At:

www.ctupublishinggroup.com/starving-artist-fund.html

Creative Talents Unleashed

Get Connected With Us!

Website: Creative Talents Unleashed Publishing Group

www.ctupublishinggroup.com

Facebook: Get connected with us on our Facebook Page

www.Facebook.com/Creativetalentsunleashed

Twitter: https://twitter.com/CTUPublishing

Blog: www.creativetalentunleashed.com

Pinterest: https://www.pinterest.com/creativetalents/

Instagram: https://instagram.com/ctupublishinggroup/

Tumbler: http://creativetalentsunleashed.tumblr.com/

Creative Talents Unleashed

Creative Talents Unleashed is an independent publishing group that offers writers an opportunity to share their writing talents with the world. We are committed to fostering and honoring the work of writers of all cultures. Our publishing group offers writing tips to assist writers in continued growth and learning, daily writing prompts and challenges to keep the writers mind sharp and challenged, marketing and events, as well as a variety of yearly publishing opportunities. We are honored to be assisting writers in the journey of becoming published authors.

www.ctupublishinggroup.com

For More Information Contact:

Creativetalentsunleashed@aol.com

www.ingramcontent.com/pod-product-compliance
Lightning Source LLC
Chambersburg PA
CBHW081013040426
42444CB00014B/3186